Lost Flowers

by

PERRY D. SULLIVAN

Dedication

All of life is but a path through time—an adventure filled with the hardships and blessings that challenge and reward. Even if one lives for many years, life is all too short. I've always thought that I would need at least 300 years simply to enjoy life's beauty—beauty that, for the most part, comes from the people who make life worth living: those who challenge, those who inspire, those who are different, and especially those whom I love. It's been said that if you have one good friend in your life, you are blessed. I've been blessed many times over and would like to dedicate this book to several people whom I love and cherish. Most of all, I give thanks to God.

First, to my old friend Jim Steckenrider. Jim showed a great deal of compassion by giving me the life-changing opportunity to race motorcycles so many years ago. Throughout our lives, we have remained close friends, and I still call upon him for advice and wisdom.

To my wonderful and kind mother, who endured incredible hardships in raising two children in a difficult environment. She laid a foundation of goodness as she nurtured me from birth onward throughout my life.

To my beautiful wife, Joanie, the mother of our children, who has held steadfast and true through many years of marriage. Her guidance, patience, and support are an incredible gift. She has remained the most important person in my life. In my opinion, she could have done much better in life than to cast her lot with mine, but I am so grateful that she has stuck with me.

To my two beloved sons, Josh Perry and John Percy, who make life interesting every day. I see my own early traits in them as they remind me of my own childhood. They are the living reminders that "Ole Percy" lives on even though he has been gone for many years. It is my hope that they use this book as a history of their heritage and that they take to heart the lessons that I pass on.

To the late Scott Flowers, a childhood and lifelong friend who embraced life and enjoyed it to the fullest.

And special thanks to my editor, Ellen, and to all who believed in this book and made it possible.

Finally, I also dedicate this book to all the victims and survivors of this true story. May you find peace.

Table of Contents

Prologue

"Hey, you fellas want a drank? You need to look over there in that cooler and get one. This one here, well it quit cooling the other day so all the dranks are over there so they'll stay cold."

We had just come in from a long morning's fox hunt, just as we had done so many times before. It was time for a cola, some potted meat, pork and beans, and crackers. We'd remembered seeing the general store and gas station when we drove past it earlier in the morning going from one field to the other listening to the walker hounds run a red fox. We pulled into the dirt parking lot beside the wooden-plank store in the custom-built dog truck. I noticed that the common-type gas pumps in front of the store were like the ones at our own country store. One read Hi-Test and the other Regular. Between them was a Wolf's Head Oil sign.

He waited for me at the bottom of the three plain wooden steps that rested on the dirt and motioned me to go on into the store ahead of him. A NuGrape metal sign was nailed to the bare wooden floor by the entrance, apparently covering a hole. As we entered the store, the clerk noticed me first.

"Who's this young man here you got with you?" the clerk asked in a slow, Southern drawl.

"He's the last button off Ole Gabe's coat," he said. "Yea, he's the last one."

"Well, looks like you got a good helper," the clerk said.

We'd made our way to the soda cooler when the clerk informed us that it had quit cooling. We moved to the other one and got us a couple of 6½-ounce Coca-Colas. We searched the counter and found a can of potted meat for him and a can of pork and beans for me, along with some saltine crackers for the both of us.

The clerk seemed curious as we approached the counter.

"Y'all part of that fox hunt going on? Some men came by earlier and said them dogs were tearing a fox up. Said it was some of the best fox racing that they ever heard."

"Yea-uh, we heard um running. They shaw was tearing that fox's ass up," he said.

The clerk was still curious, nosy even. "Y'all from round here?"

"Naw, we from North Carolina. Johnston County," he said.

"Oh, yeah, I heard of that area. I use to buy whiskey from round there. I use to buy it from a man named Percy Flowers."

I looked up at him, and he looked down at me, smiled, and nodded slightly, a gesture that I should just remain quiet.

"Oh yea-uh, I heard of that fella, Percy Flowers. You

said you knowed him?" he asked the clerk.

"Yeah, I use to buy whiskey from him, knowed him good."

He remained quiet, pulled out a round wad of cash held together with a rubber band, peeled off a couple of bills, paid for the items, and walked back with me to the truck. We sat on the extended steel tailgate to enjoy our Cokes and food.

"Why didn't you tell him who you are?" I asked him.

"Well, he did say he knowed me." He chuckled.

Percy Flowers was by far one of the most notorious moonshiners who ever lived. His life of moonshining began at a young age—just after he ran away from home for a night to escape the harshness of a hard-edged and abusive father, who had that very day snapped a tobacco stick across Percy's back for not following his instructions.

That fateful night, Percy stumbled upon an old Negro making whiskey in the woods and struck a deal that would set the course of his life. Through illicit whiskey sales, Percy built up an empire that dominated four to five thousand acres of some of the finest farmland in North Carolina. There he farmed cotton, tobacco, corn, and soybeans, a complement to and cover for the real business of making whiskey.

It is said that in his heyday, Percy Flowers could not walk into a restaurant without people pointing and whispering. Folks from all over the East Coast wanted to be associated with him and went so far as to pretend to know him personally.

It is said that he made millions of dollars selling whiskey.

It is also said that people actually killed to protect Percy. Not out of fear but loyalty. The Feds tried for decades to charge Percy with illegal whiskey making but could never get a conviction by a jury of his peers.

Percy also had a love for foxhound racing and perfected the best foxhound bloodlines in the world. He participated in and won National Field Trial hunts and became a legend among fox hunters and breeders. He also excelled in game-cock fighting and produced world-renowned Red and Grey fighting cock bloodlines.

Overall, Percy was a driven man and achieved whatever he committed himself to. According to a *Saturday Evening Post* article in 1958, Percy was "the most notorious moonshiner in all of the United States." Although the federal government tried for years to convict him for his large-scale moonshining operations, they never could quite get the job done. Percy evaded and avoided prosecution, both through sheer luck and a network of friendly or frightened magistrates and law enforcement authorities who were willing or well paid to look the other way.

He mingled among the wealthy and powerful—senators, generals, and captains of industry. But he enjoyed the hard-working, salt-of-the-earth people most. After all, he'd grown up dirt poor and earned every penny he ever made. He was known as a man you could trust. When he gave you his word, it was as good as gold. He was a chivalrous warrior, a generous philanthropist.

No other man who ever lived had more of an appetite or love for life and respect for heritage than Percy Flowers.

During his lifetime, he amassed an empire of thousands

of acres mentioned in just a few short words in his will at his life's end.

Percy's son had been killed years earlier in a tragic plane crash and his obituary stated that his wife and daughter survived him. It seemed his life and legacy had nearly come to the end.

Percy's death closed the door on an empire that had thrived for many years. All the foxhounds and fighting cocks were auctioned off upon his death. The country store that had been noted as the brain center for his operation was rebuilt and refashioned into a legitimate, respectable business. Many of the characters of his day moved away and were mostly forgotten.

But not everything wrapped up so neatly. Percy's untimely death left unfinished business among his clan. He was unable to follow through with an old secret that he'd started in May of 1962—a secret many whispered about but few spoke of openly. Percy's stern words to his lover's husband would seal that man's lips and would void the man's heart of all love or affection, leaving him to work nearly all of his life empty, hopeless, and broken. Percy's actions would affect many lives and produce deeply scarred victims while propagating a long and renowned bloodline for generations after his death. He left behind some of his own children alone, homeless, troubled, and ill prepared for what lay ahead.

Introduction

It was an early morning in July as I piloted the commercial MD-80 aircraft past 33,000 feet to 34,000 feet. We had just left LaGuardia International Airport, New York, en route to Dallas/Fort Worth. We leveled the aircraft and performed the "cruise checklist." I noted the ground speed, around 410, with light winds at altitude. It was a pleasant, mostly clear morning with the distant horizon in view. A few clouds drifted to the south but they were not in our flight path. I turned the autopilot on and the auto throttles began to retard slightly in order to hold a constant speed of 0.76 Mach. The other pilot asked me where I was from.

"The St. Louis area. St. Charles. Just by the Missouri River. What about you?"

He replied, "North Carolina. Apex. Do you know that area?"

"Some," I said.

If only you knew.

A sense of pride of place overwhelmed me as my spirit became set afire with thoughts of my childhood. *I knew the area before you ever thought about it.* I owned that area by right of the king who'd established and ruled his own kingdom, built his land up, and made it a spot on the map before any of you newcomers moved there or had ever even heard of it.

I was born out of a married woman's yearning to bear children and the king's willingness to fulfill her need. From the moment I was conceived on a sweat-covered mattress sheet one hot August summer day, the two of them passionately embraced and plotted their illicit affair.

By a modern-day *droit du seigneur*, the king would lay claim to a subject's womb and in so doing propagate his line across the generations.

On that steamy day in 1961, the king and my mother married their flesh, conceived me, and I was born in May of 1962. In December 1964, a second child, my sister, was also conceived between the two lovers.

Two illegitimate children, as illegal in the eyes of the world as moonshine and also as real and full of fire. His blood flows through my veins and has fueled my searching soul as I carry on his spirit. By that blood right I tell you this story through a series of letters to my two sons, Josh Perry and John Percy, so that their heritage is not forever lost. These letters are my personal testimony and revelation of the events surrounding the life of this notorious moonshiner and his legacy that has been lost for so many years.

1

THE MOONSHINE KING

Dear Josh and John,

There was once a man who was legend and lore. He lived east of Clayton, North Carolina, where he became a figure of near-mythical status. He was known far and wide for his large-scale, illegal moonshining activities. All of the old-timers talk of him as a Robin Hood who gave back to the community by helping churches and the common man. At the same time, this local legend was a warrior, fierce and formidable against anyone who crossed him. Throughout his career and conquests, he amassed thousands of acres of land where he farmed cotton, tobacco, corn, wheat, and soybeans. The money he earned from farming and moon-shining allowed him to pursue his real passions: cockfighting and foxhound racing. He was well known for breeding the world's finest fighting cocks and foxhounds. It is said that his notoriety in North Carolina is second only to that of actress Ava Gardner. He is now a legend and folk hero, a figure everyone wants to be associated with in some way. When you visit the area, all kinds of people seem to have known him personally and like to tell his stories.

But the king had a secret and a few stories that only I know. The first story I'll share with you reveals who the king really was, how he came to moonshining, and why these stories are so important for you two boys. This story is straight from the king's lips as he told it directly to me as a boy.

The year was 1913. The smell of fresh dirt wafted from the ground where a single-mule plow furrowed the hard earth. A boy, not more than ten years old, walked behind an old black work mule, pulling on the long plow lines to keep the animal straight in the field. He wore an old shirt along with knee pants made from a burlap seed bag. The boy felt the cool earth under his bare feet as he avoided the larger, hard dirt clods. The sun began to rise over the treetops and he appreciated its warmth on his back and side—a pleasant relief from the early-morning coolness. Typical for an early Carolina morning, a thin layer of fog hovered over the field. As the mule's hoofs stomped the dirt, the old wooden-handled steel plow creaked, burrowing down in the dirt three or four inches. Several blackbirds flew past overhead. To his right he beheld his long shadow cast upon the earth, a silent companion during his hours of hard labor. His small footprints trod the same path as generations of his forefathers and the sweat from his brow moistened the same tobacco fields.

The boy's days were filled with hard physical labor. His father, "Ole Man Josh," had "snapped the whip" and kept the young boy busy. At just ten or eleven years of age, he was expected to work just like any full-grown man, and he did so without complaint. Watching the sun rise and set while walking behind a mule was just a normal day. When not plowing, he attended to the many other farm chores expected of him.

But in his sixteenth year, his life would veer sharply away from that of his family.

The sun went down on yet another hot summer day and the now-strapping teenager worked until sunset, looping the large green tobacco leaves onto a wooden looping horse. He placed one tobacco stick after another into the "V" on the wooden horse. The hired hands would then wrap the leaf ends with string and form the sticks of tobacco that would be placed in the wooden plank barns for wood-fired curing. Ole Man Josh walked over and glanced at the stick pile to discover only a few tobacco sticks remaining. He glowered at his son sternly.

"Run up to the house and git sum mo' backer sticks," he said.

The young man started walking toward the house when he was caught by a terrific blow across his back that nearly dropped him to his knees. He turned around and saw his father standing over him with a tobacco stick in hand.

"Boy, I toll yuh ta run. And when I say run, I mean break A TROT!"

The boy glared up at his towering father and turned away. "You've hit me the last time, you sumbitch," he hissed through clenched teeth.

Ole Josh lunged forward, hand raised and ready to strike again. The youth scrambled to his feet and sprinted toward the thick woods without looking back. He sped across the field, some two hundred feet, and made it to the woods' edge. He took shelter in the tree-lined cover, diving behind a large log lying on the ground. Sliding himself under the edge of the log, he heard Ole Man Josh yelling for him.

"You git back here now, ya hear!"

The boy remained quiet and tried to quell his panting. He could hear his own heart beating as his father yelled at him. It was nearly dark and quiet settled across the woods. The tall oaks formed a cover and it was darker in the woods than in the field. He rose slowly from behind the log to find that the coast was clear. The boy knew the area like the back of his hand. Making it to a nearby dirt path beyond the trees, he started the mile-long walk to his uncle's house.

As he came upon a small creek running parallel to the path, he noticed a flicker of light deep in the woods. Not sure what he had just seen, he stopped and peered into the darkness. Again he saw the light flicker. Curiosity got the better of him and he parted the weeds alongside the creek with his arms and stepped off the path. The large hardwood trees surrounded him and he stood still, focusing on the flickering light. Hunched over, he crept forward. The light grew brighter as he inched his way closer. He knew the creek bent around and ran back to the place where the flicker came from. He crossed the creek, careful not to stumble on the loose pebbles and small rocks in the creek bed. By now, the moon had risen and shone its light through the dense forest. He could clearly see the water running over the creek bed. The gurgling of the running creek water covered his footfalls as he crossed to the other side. Moving slowly toward the light, he spied a person walking around some barrels. These barrels he recognized—he'd seen them before. Next to the barrels was the familiar shape of a whiskey still.

As he inched ever closer, an old Negro who had been leaning over a barrel suddenly rose up, face taut with suspicion. The boy recognized him and called out his name. Startled, the old Negro jumped up and peered through the darkness to see the source of the noise.

"Who dat?" he cried out.

The boy walked slowly out of the dense woods and again hailed the Negro by name.

"Hey, Lester!"

Lester was surprised to see the boy. "Say boy, what's you out dis time a night fo'? You 'pose ta be home. I'm gonna tell Ole Man Josh when I see 'im."

Quickly the boy snapped back, "I'm gone tell dat you here, too. Now you ain't gone say nuthin' are you?"

Over the next few minutes, the young boy would drive a devil's deal that would set his life's course. Looking back at this moment from the vantage point of a life fully lived, he would say that at that moment he stood at the "crossroads of life," making a momentous choice about which direction to take. Perhaps he was talking to Old Nick himself. Or perhaps the Almighty was lending a hand that would later change so many lives. In any case, the boy made his choice and would never look back.

"Lester, I want you to learn me how to make whiskey. If you do, den I won't say nuthin'. I'll jus' work here and be quiet."

Lester looked at him silently, rubbing his chin. He considered this for a few moments, and replied, "All right, but yuh betta not say a word, boy."

The two of them turned and walked toward the whiskey still and mash barrels, and Lester began to teach him the ways of moonshine whiskey making.

Under that moonlit night deep in the Carolina forest, a mighty king had been born. Joshua Percy Flowers's first lesson in moonshining had commenced.

Joshua Percy Flowers as a boy

Over the next year, Percy worked with Lester, learning how to make and sell whiskey. He learned all he could about the ins and outs of "the business," for—illegal or not—a business it was. Moonshining was hard work, but the demand for corn whiskey was high and the money flowed. Within that year, the boy would buy all of Lester's gear—still, barrels, and all. Percy soon employed Lester to make the whiskey and focused himself on selling it and building his tax-free empire.

Within a few short years, he had made quite the name for himself. People liked his smooth, clear, potent hooch and came from miles around to buy it. They also liked dealing with Percy, understanding that he was a man of the people who understood and related to their ways and hardships having lived them himself. He, too, had been poor and had done his share of suffering. Percy steadily saved money and expanded his moonshining business. But as his fortune and operations grew, so did his notoriety with local authorities.

One day Lester reported to Percy that some stranger had been snooping around his barrels of mash at the still. Fresh footprints were visible around the soft ground by the barrels and it looked like some of the mash was missing. Lester believed that some local boys had been stealing the mash and drinking it. Percy, armed with a single-barrel, twelve-gauge shotgun, slipped down to the mash barrels several times during the next few nights. On one such occasion, he discovered a man leaning over one of the barrels. He raised his shotgun and took aim at the mash thief's backside. As he squeezed the trigger, the twelve-gauge let out a bang that echoed through the woods. The mash thief fell beside the barrels onto the ground and grabbed the back of his pants. He rose to his feet and turned to face his shooter. Percy was shocked to see that the mash thief was the sheriff! Before the officer could take a step, Percy turned and fled into the woods. Within a few hours, his first whiskey still had been seized and destroyed by local authorities.

During the 1920s and throughout the Great Depression, Percy continued to make whiskey and build a loyal customer base. By the mid-1930s, he even operated a small tavern in Smithfield on Highway 301, at the site of the present-day White Swan Bar-B-Q. He and his brother Jim ran the joint together. Howard, a young Negro boy, worked with them, selling the king's "white lightning." Howard stuffed the glass pints of corn whiskey in his knee boots and sold it to the locals who came by. Percy once said much later that he made more money in the 1930s than he ever had since.

By the end of the 1930s, Percy had begun to purchase farmland and later built a new store. He sold his tavern and continued his moonshining operation while also expanding into farming. Farming and moonshining were symbiotic: Percy grew his own corn for mash and then marketed the whiskey from his store. Long before business schools were teaching the concept, Percy Flowers was actually creating "synergy" between his business divisions. The sheer size of the land—eventually encompassing thousands of acres—was very effective in hiding Percy's whiskey operations. He needed the land, both for security from the Feds and for future expansion.

Percy also loved foxhound racing and cockfighting and used his whiskey money to develop the best bloodline of foxhounds and gamecocks in the country.

By the 1950s, Percy Flowers was a high-rolling whiskey millionaire. He owned dozens of new Cadillacs through the years. He also loved fast automobiles and in the 1940s had custom-built Fords equipped with high-powered Cadillac engines.

*Joshua Percy Flowers with one
of his many Cadillacs
(in front of the Sullivan home)*

By this time, Percy's wide circle of influence included those who worked for him directly and those legitimate authorities who knew about the whiskey making but politely looked the other way. This made him virtually immune from the law. His whiskey flowed like water. He sold cases by the truckload and shipped them up and down the eastern seaboard. Names like Parker, Gooch, and Sugar Daddy all worked the towering whiskey stills deep under the cover of Percy's protection.

By the 1950s and '60s, Percy was notorious—he had been the target of federal agents for some thirty years. They had tried many times over to convict him of making illegal whiskey only to come up short on any substantive charges. The federal and state governments attempted many times to close in on him, but there wasn't a court in the land that could convict him of making whiskey. The plain truth was that, among a jury of his peers—the common people—Percy was untouchable, a sort of moonshine Robin Hood. Everyone knew of his good deeds outside of whiskey making.

Even though the Feds could not achieve a whiskey conviction, they eventually managed a tax conviction, estimating his earnings and turning up the pressure by charging for back taxes. To meet this debt, Percy was forced to sell timber from his many farms. The constant federal pressure to break his will began to take a toll as he aged. At the height of his reign, Percy owned between four and five thousand acres of the finest land in North Carolina, all just east of Clayton. He continued his operation at a much-reduced pace through the 1970s and up until his death in 1982.

According to genealogy databases, Percy descended from a long line of Flowers dating back to England. His forefathers can be traced back as early as 1525 AD to John Flower and Sybil Hale of Poterne, Wiltshire, England. In 1666, Jacob Flower, from Middlesex, England, boldly voyaged to the New World. Hc and his wife, Hardy, continued the distinguished Flower bloodline in America. Henry Edmund Flower, the first Flower born in America, lived in Surry County, Virginia. Over the next six generations, the Flower clan migrated to North Carolina. They were hard-working tobacco farmers, slave owners, and clever businessmen. Percy was from a long line of fierce survivors who'd weathered some of the hardest of times and still flourished.

As with all mortals, however, even Percy's days were numbered. When his heart failed and his days were nearing an end, he clung to life right down to his last breath. He knew that he had unfinished business that would leave hardship among his clan. His last will and testament stated simply that everything would be left to his beloved wife. His only legitimate son had been killed in a dreadful airplane crash in the 1950s. His surviving spouse and daughter were left to struggle to hold onto the farm and keep it from the grasping eyes and hands of the tax collectors. The king's obituary listed very few survivors. It seems the story should end here, but it doesn't.

My sons, I write you this letter to finally reveal an old secret I've harbored for many decades. My true identity was only known by a few and was kept a closely guarded secret. Throughout my life, I have listened to people tell of

Percy Flowers and how life was on the farm and how they knew him so well. I quietly and politely listened and just nodded in agonizing shame as my true identity and pain went unnoticed.

Mr. Joshua Percy Flowers was my father and your grandfather. His blood is the very blood that runs through our veins. This secret must be told to set straight the record of his legacy. I never had any claim to financial inheritance due to my illegitimacy, yet my identity was well known among our clan. I was there with my father during all of his later years as I grew up on the farm and at the store. My identity was hidden from many folks, and I was known to many as Beatrice and Willis's boy. But, in fact, I am the last direct bloodline son of Joshua Percy Flowers. I knew him as my real father, even though I had to pretend to be someone else in order to keep the peace and prevent public humiliation for many.

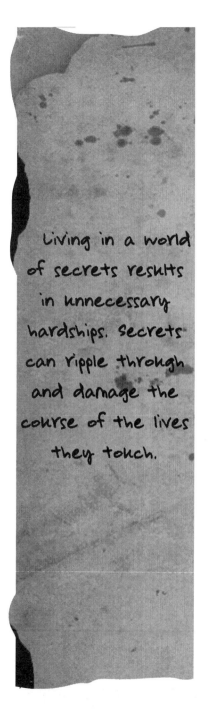

Living in a world of secrets results in unnecessary hardships. Secrets can ripple through and damage the course of the lives they touch.

After my father's death, I was troubled with this truth—this secret—for years. All I have left is the true story of Joshua Percy Flowers as I knew him as a man and a father. This is the time to let you know who he really was and who you are. As you grow up, you will hear many stories about him. Let me offer you a firsthand account of your grandfather, as told by his son, your father. I have taken all precautions to ensure that you grow up in a normal home free from secrets. Living in a world of secrets results in unnecessary hardships. Secrets can ripple through and damage the course of the lives they touch. It is my hope for you boys to have better lives and fewer hardships than I did, God willing.

*Percy Flowers holding his son,
Perry Sullivan, in 1963*

Percy Flowers at the Sullivan home on Motorcycle Road

2

THE LAST BUTTON OFF OLE GABE'S COAT

Dear Josh and John,

It is important that you know how much you are loved, needed, and cared for. The first years of a person's life, I believe, are critical. Your surroundings may not always sparkle with glitter from material gain and riches, but your life can always be filled with hope, compassion, and love if you are nurtured from a young age. Let me tell you about the early years on the farm and how it all started for me...

Beatrice, or Bea as she was called, lay on her back, legs in stirrups, moaning and groaning the pains of childbirth in a dimly lit delivery room at the Woodard Herring Hospital in Wilson, North Carolina. To her these were pains of complete joy—pains that only a first-time mother could describe. Her forehead shone with a glaze of sweat as she endured the agonizing labor contractions. Beside her, holding her hand, was her lifelong friend and cousin Polly, her only reassurance that all would be well. Bea's husband, Willis, who went by the name Curry, was absent from the most important event of her life. While she bore that first child, he remained at the Flowers country store, working, head held down, and muttering contempt.

Beatrice Sullivan (left) and her sister, Sylvia, in the 1960s

Polly, friend of Bea, holding Perry Sullivan in 1962 at the Flowers Store

Beatrice (Bea) and Willis
(Curry) Sullivan

Curry was filled with the fear and hatred of knowing what he knew and what he would have to do. What he knew was that yet another secret would threaten his very life and livelihood forever. He was not equipped or skilled enough to negotiate an alternative to this lifelong sentence.

Bea had wanted children for over fifteen years. She and Curry had tried repeatedly, but the mumps had gone down on him and they were unable to conceive. Although still living under the same roof, their marriage had become strained and they'd grown distant. As the years passed and age took its toll, Bea knew her chances for motherhood were nearing an end. She had often prayed to God to grant her children.

Bea and Curry were country people, just getting by as so many did during those hard times. Curry worked for Percy at the country store and helped tend to the foxhounds. They lived on a dirt path just off Buffalo Road east of Clayton.

It was 1967 and I was just five years old. I was that child Bea had prayed for so often and waited so long for. Our home was an old, wood-plank country house with creaking wooden floors and loose windows that shook and rattled when the thunder crashed. The fact was that Percy actually owned this house where my family lived and he visited us almost daily. It was hot in the humid North Carolina summer and freezing in the winter. We had a big draw fan in the kitchen at the rear of the house and the front door stayed open to let the fan pull a draft through the house to help keep it cooler on the hot summer days. The back porch was screened in, and that was where the old folks sat when they visited.

Just outside the house was a pump house made of cinder blocks. Curry went in there often to work on the pump. It always seemed cool and moist inside and the ground stayed damp. There were usually large brown spiders that crawled on the inside block walls. The pump was electric with two large wheels connected by a pulley belt. An electric wire hung over the pump connected to the pump with black monkey tape. The big wheel wobbled and squeaked as it turned. The pump house door was held shut by a piece of wood that rotated on a nail through the center, forming a latch. The hole in the latch was hollowed out from where the latch had been opened so many times.

Behind the house was an old barn where my Shetland pony, Bill, was stabled. Beside the barn were two wooden buildings that were always full of one-gallon and half-gallon glass jars and some broken cases of club soda—at least that's what Mama said was in the jars. I think it might have been whiskey, since people were always talking about the whiskey made around there.

One night we heard a loud explosion.

"It's da law blowing up a still over in them woods," Curry explained.

Slightly below the house and down a small hill was a slaughterhouse with a big walk-in freezer, a smokehouse room for salted hams, and a large vat with a long, steel pipe arm that the men pulled on to raise a steel vat. This was where the hogs were killed every winter by all the hired old Negros who wore black rubber boots for the job. Beside the slaughterhouse was a hog pen with a concrete floor and wooden-rail sides made from two-by-fours where a man shot the hogs in the forehead with a .22 just before the other men sliced their throats with butcher knives and bled them out. The concrete floor was stained with hog blood—it was always bright red when it came out of the hog's head and neck but black when it dried up on the floor or ground. They would drag the hogs to a vat of scalding water, throw them in, and use Mason jar lids and grubbing hoes to scrape off the animals' hair. Then they hung them by their hind legs, high up, in a three-legged tripod made of small trees. They cut open the full length of the hog's belly with a butcher knife, spilling the smelly guts and organs onto the ground or into a large steel tub. I don't know much about what they did next except that they moved the hogs into the slaughterhouse and cut them up in little pieces. The bare, raw meat lay on the long wooden tables where they prepared it for the store. The old Negros poured salt on the table and with large bare hands rubbed the salt on the hams. Then they hung the hams in the smokehouse. There was a large, silver metal meat grinder that sat on another table and made a whining noise when it ran. The men fed the meat into the funnel-shaped top and it bulged out the small holes on the side of the grinder. They called that the sausage meat. They saved the intestinal linings and stuffed the sausage meat into them. We always had a lot of hog meat. Two large black iron pots sat outside mounted over a wood fire. Smoke from the fire rose up over the sides of the pots. One Negro always had the job of poking the fire with a charred stick and adding pieces of wood to keep it burning. His name was Lung. Hog fat bubbled inside the pots to be made into cooking lard or box lye soap. They also cooked chitlins and cracklins. A man at the store once said, "Dem niggers like chitlins, don't they?" The old black men worked hard. One of them sang a song and sometimes another one would join in and sing, too.

In the yard was a small pen made from wooden soda crates. The crates were stacked on top of each other, five high, making a puppy pen about as big as a bedroom. Some of the crates had Mountain Dew printed on them. I couldn't read, but I knew what Mountain Dew was when I saw it. In the pen were several puppies. Percy had warned me not to mess with the old Walker hound bitch because she might bite me. I knew the old bitch was the mama dog with the big saggy titties. The puppies liked to feed from her. I played with the puppies and rubbed their fat bellies.

On the opposite side of the slaughterhouse was another large fenced open area for the dogs, probably three or four acres. This was where the foxhounds always were, unless we went fox hunting with them. In that case, Percy would come by and select the dogs for the hunt. Percy would talk to the dog man and say, "Bring out that July bitch with the high-pitched, squealing mouth and that dog with all the drive that's always at the front of the hunt." Sometimes we left four or five of the hounds behind because Percy said "they ain't worth a shit" or "they're run out from the last hunt and need to rest." Whatever their condition, he would know.

The dog man would bring cow guts and chicken feet in a large aluminum-back truck for the dogs to eat. The guts were poured onto the ground from the back of the truck out of fifty-gallon steel drums. The brakes squealed as he stopped the big truck. He'd hop up onto the truck bed and then struggle with the weight of the drum as he moved it to the edge of the tall tailgate. He tilted the drum and the cow guts splashed out on the ground with a sloshing sound. The hungry hounds would form a circle around the first torrent of guts poured out, tearing, ripping, and chewing away. Dogs being what they are, sometimes they fought over the slimy viscera. I would gingerly pick my way around the dogs, trying to stay clear so I wouldn't get bitten. I could barely stand the stench of the raw cow guts, but the dogs certainly didn't mind. To them it must have smelled like the finest meal ever. I walked behind the truck and used a ten-penny nail to poke holes in the guts to hear the air seep out. The entrails made a *sssshhhhhh* sound as they slowly deflated like balloons.

I had a backwoods childhood, even for a country boy. Mama would say, "Go outside," and I was happy to oblige. I spent most of my day just playing. Sometimes I found large spiders on the pump house wall or in the slaughterhouse and tried to hit them with a rock. From the weeds that grew beside the slaughterhouse there were a lot of writing spiders, or banana spiders, that seemed to scribble on their webs. Their bodies were huge with greenish yellow on their backs. Their legs were pointy and as long as popsicle sticks. I was careful not to fall when I leaned over their webs and tried to read their cryptic messages. I could never read what they wrote. I couldn't read anyways, so I would just make something up. Mama said they wouldn't hurt me, so I just took her word on that. I liked finding toads, too. Mama said that frogs would give you warts if they peed on you, so I was careful not to get peed on.

In front of the old house was a small, dusty, and over-grown dirt path leading to Buffalo Road. Grass grew in the middle of the path between the wheel tracks. When it didn't rain for a few days, you could see the dust trail of a truck coming down the path before you could see the truck. I liked walking barefooted on the sandy path and drag-ging my foot through the sand. Blackberry bushes, plum trees, and weeds lined both sides of the path. During the summer, fresh blackberries and plums abounded. Mama walked with me to pick them, putting them in a brown pa-per sack. The problem was the red bugs—what some folks call the "chiggers." I got a lot of red bugs when picking the blackberries and plums. They made pink welts and itched real bad. Mama put a drop of fingernail polish on the pink welts. She said that it would kill the red bugs. Sometimes I had red fingernail polish spots all over me and looked like I had some kind of weird tropical disease. I didn't care. I still liked to pick blackberries and plums. You had to know which ones to pick so you didn't get a sour-un, and I knew which ones were just right—the soft ones.

We also had outdoor yard dogs that were not part of the foxhounds. These dogs just "took up" at our house and stayed there. The dogs barked and ran down the road to meet cars and trucks. But the only cars and trucks that ever came down our road belonged to the Dog Man and to Percy and Curry.

Percy came by almost every day. When his big Cadillac came down the road, the dogs barked and Mama ran to look out the window. "Percy is here!" she'd yell out to us. She liked it when he came by. Curry never came home until nighttime, when we were asleep. He worked all day, and I hardly saw him. He never spent any time with us as I remember. So, odds were, it was the dog man or Percy when a truck came down the road.

We loved Percy. He owned all the land around there. He just about always drove a big Cadillac with fins on the back fenders. In fact, that's how I learned to drive, sitting in his lap and steering the big Cadillac while he worked the pedals. I really liked the Cadillac because it had air conditioning and smelled like a cigar. I held my head by the air vent to feel the cool air blow across my face, smelling the cigar smoke mixed with the air-conditioning air. That smell memory is still vivid to this day. I was also fascinated by the Cadillac's electric windows. No other car had these, and Percy let me run them up and down by pushing the little silver tabs on each door. The large windows made a *hmmm* sound when they went up and down. The line was drawn at blowing the horn—I wasn't allowed to blow the horn much as it made the dogs bark.

In the ashtray was a photo of a pretty girl with blond hair. One day, I picked up the picture.

"Who is it?" I asked Percy.

"That's your half sister, Becky. You can keep it."

What's a half sister? I thought.

Percy always made big of me and my "whole" sister, Tammy. When he came by, he talked, gooched me, and bounced me on his knee. He brought us Coca-Colas and candy when he came over.

Mama would say, "You know dat's your daddy, don't you?"

She always said it. I guess she forgot I already knew.

One day Percy came by and went to Mama's bedroom. The bedroom had two separate doors, one leading to the living room and the other one opening into the other bedroom. They locked the door and I couldn't get in from the living room. I went to the other door and peeked through the skeleton keyhole but couldn't see anything. Good thing that lock was on my side of the door. I pressed the small lock tab and unlocked the door and opened it. Percy was standing beside the bed in front of Mama and he was missing his brim hat. He never took off his brim hat. Mama had to peek her head around him to see me. They looked surprised. I guess I was too.

The summer ended, and it was Christmas time. You know what you know and that's what you know when you're five years old.

I knew that Christmas was fun and that Santa Claus came and brought toys and candy. I stood in the living room looking through the window across a bare field. Behind me was an old fuel oil heater with a large black pipe that ran up to the ceiling. I felt the cold coming from the window as I blew my breath onto it to scribble something with my finger. The wind blew through the cracks around the edge of the windows and I felt its iciness coming in. My sister, Tammy, was sitting on the floor playing. The old black and white Zenith TV on its metal frame roller was on. Mama came from the kitchen and told us that Santa Claus was coming soon.

I spun around at her words and started asking when. I asked her every day if Santa would come that night. When it got close to Christmas we just knew. Mama said it was time to hang our Christmas stockings. She went into Curry's sock drawer and got me and Tammy a large sock each to hang up for Santa Claus.

We always got up early to check our Christmas socks. Every year we got apples, oranges, nuts, and candy, along with a toy. Today's children might see fruit as a punishment, but we were delighted. Funny thing—the oranges, apples, nuts, and candy looked just like the ones at the store. Mama had been cooking cakes. She always baked good cakes, but her Christmas cakes were special. She put a nut bowl on the coffee table so we had nuts at Christmas. There was a silver-handled nutcracker that stood up in the nut tray. It was good to get to the nut tray right away, 'cause in a few days just the shells would be left and all the good nuts would be gone.

Curry worked at the store when he wasn't tending to the foxhounds. All kinds of salesmen left Santa Claus calendars at the store, but the Coca-Cola man brought the best ones. His showed Santa Claus leaning back with a big smile, holding a Coca-Cola. I liked the picture but didn't understand the calendar numbers then. The smaller 6½-ounce Coca-Colas had Santa Claus on them. Anyways, Mountain Dew was still my favorite.

At the store there were chocolate-covered peanuts, chocolate-covered cherries, candy orange slices, orange marshmallow candy, and apples and oranges by the boxful. The candy didn't melt in the winter because it was so cold.

Another salesman left some new radios. Curry got one and brought it home for Christmas. It was red with gold-colored dials and a pull-up chrome antenna. The outside was like red plastic alligator skin—it looked nice. Curry also brought home some drinking glasses that he said came out of the bubble gum boxes. We had a collection of the red glasses with gold trim. They looked fancy. Along with our grape jelly glasses we had a lot of drinking glasses.

On Christmas morning in 1966, Curry was working at Percy's store as he did every Christmas. Mama said that Percy would be by. The dogs started barking and we heard a car pull up. Mama ran to the back door and yelled that Percy was here and we better come see him. We raced to the door as Mama opened it and told him to come on in. He had a ham and a carton of small Coca-Colas in his hands, and he placed them on the kitchen table as we followed him to the living room. Mama asked him if he wanted something to eat. He thought for a moment and asked if she had "any of them biscuits." She said yes and went to get them. As he sat down, he asked me and Tammy what we had been doing. We both scampered onto his lap as he pulled us up and placed us on his knees. We were excited to see him. It was the best part of the day. Mama came back into the room with biscuits and they started eating and talking.

I asked Mama if I could get Percy his gift. Without waiting for an answer, I scrambled down off his lap and raced to the exact spot under the aluminum-foil Christmas tree where I had placed the gift. That year I had gone to the dime store and shopped long and hard to find him a perfect gift. I finally picked out some Hai Karate aftershave for him. Of course I'd inspected all the aftershaves before settling on the Hai Karate. Racing back to the couch, I held the gift up to him. He took it and said, "Let's see here what you got?"

Perry and Tammy, Christmas, 1966

Perry Sullivan as a young child in the old Radio Flyer wagon (in background some of Percy Flowers's foxhounds)

Percy started to unwrap the gift, and I was so excited I could hardly wait. Old folks took a long time to open their gifts!

He inspected the bottle and exclaimed, "Yes sar, that's some good stuff right there." As he twisted the black cap open, I leaned over to smell the top of the green, liquid-filled bottle. It smelled strong and fragrant. Percy put a little in his hands, rubbed them together, and slapped them to his face a couple of times. He smiled big as he reached out and wrapped his arms around me. I knew what would come next. He brushed his lightly bearded face against my cheeks. I squiggled and squirmed because it was so rough and prickly. His aftershave smelled different on his face than mine. Percy had a unique smell. I giggled and he laughed.

"Perry, you know whose boy you are, don't you? You da las' button off Ole Gabe's coat." He told me that a lot. Guess he thought I might forget it.

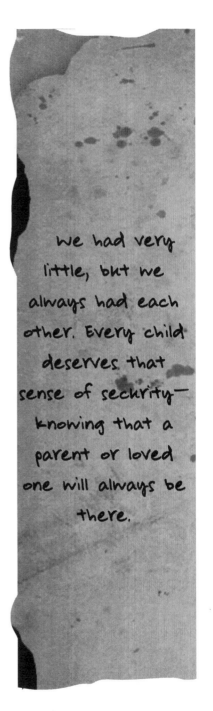

we had very little, but we always had each other. Every child deserves that sense of security—knowing that a parent or loved one will always be there.

One time I said that I was going to tell Curry whose boy I really was. Percy and Mama didn't like that and Mama said, "You better not say that now, I mean it." Somehow I knew what they meant, so I enjoyed teasing them. I knew not to say anything. Guess I learned to keep secrets early on.

That was life at the old plank house as seen through the eyes of a five-year-old boy. There was a sense of security and love that came from knowing a parent or loved one will always be there for you—regardless of the situation. And as far back as I can remember, Percy was there for me.

Percy Flowers and Perry

3

PERCY'S STORE

Dear Josh and John,

As a child, much of my time was spent at Percy's store. The store had no fancy name, just a small sign by Highway 42 that read Flowers Grocery. Everyone just knew it as Percy's store. The store was a large brick building that marked the corner of Highway 42 and Buffalo Road like the bull's-eye on a dartboard. Everybody who was anybody knew of it. The March 1958 edition of the Saturday Evening Post described Percy's store as the "brain center for the Flowers operation."

The store was where everything took place. A kid could get a penny piece of candy or moneymen could negotiate a high-dollar deal. People who worked there were as much a part of the store as the very bricks and mortar that made the walls. The store featured an ongoing circus act of characters from the comical to the political, from law-abiding to criminal.

To me, the store was like a second home. I got to know the regulars, but there were only a handful of people who were considered like family in the store. We all kept a watchful eye on the people coming and going as the whiskey sales were conducted.

The Cast

A diverse and colorful cast of characters worked at and patronized the store.

Curry ran the store full time. He was known as an honest and quiet man who would, most of the time, answer with a curt head nod or a simple reply. Curry was a slim, medium-sized man with thin gray hair brushed straight back and flat on his head. He always wore modest clothes—khaki-type pants, a button-up shirt, and a belt with a key strap from which dangled the store keys. He kept a small plastic pencil and pen holder in his shirt pocket that protected his shirt from ink and pencil marks. His face was firm and mostly serious. He was as serious and quiet at the store as he was at home.

Percy and Curry had an "understanding." Percy trusted Curry in the brain center of his operation because he knew Curry would never turn on him. Percy let Curry drive his old green double-decker dog truck back and forth to work. Curry was the only one who had a "company truck."

Percy was known to have once remarked, "Hellfire, Curry would never take a penny from nobody." He was right about that. Even though Curry had only made it through grade school, he was good with the register, and, most of all, he was trustworthy. He worked at the store for a monthly salary of just $300. Every morning, he left our house and drove the green Ford truck down the long, red-clay dirt road to arrive at the store and open by 7:00 a.m. He stood behind the register all day, every day, even weekends, until 9:00 p.m., except Thursday—his only day off. I never heard him complain, not once, not ever.

I often rode to the store with Curry and spent the day there while he worked. He never said much to me during the ride or at the store. I remember riding to the store on cool mornings and Curry would open the driver's-side window, allowing the cold wind to blow in. I shivered with cold, but he wouldn't close the window.

Even though Curry was quiet and honest, he was not perfect. He had his own secrets, faults, and foibles to deal with. At times he seemed heartless. Once when we were riding home from the store he stopped beside the road. He got out of the truck and walked to the back and opened the tailgate. I followed him out. He pulled a medium-sized cardboard box from the bed of the truck. Six small puppies, foxhounds, were in the box, and all were whimpering as if they were hungry.

"What are we doing with 'em?" I asked.

"They're mixed up and no good," he told me.

He took one out of the box and slung it against a large tree trunk, killing it. I tried to persuade him to let me have the rest of the puppies and not to hurt them. He just continued to throw them one by one against the tree and eventually killed them all. We got back into the truck and left the puppies lying dead by the tree at the edge of the woods. He sat behind the wheel and drove home, never showing one shred of emotion and never saying a word more about it. When we arrived home, I slowly walked inside as my eyes teared up. I found a quiet place and cried over what had just happened.

Joel was the "Dog Man" in charge of keeping the hundreds of foxhounds fed and watered. When he wasn't tending to the dogs, he mowed the many acres of grass inside the various dog pens. Most of the time, Joel sat around the store. He was a slim, short man who always wore brogan high-top boots and went without his shirt in the summer. His chest hair was sparsely patched, gray and long. His back and arms were tanned from the sun and freckled. He kept his hair closely cropped on his small, round head. When he smiled (or grimaced), the large gap between his two front teeth showed prominently.

Joel the Dog Man talked a lot of shit most of the time, or at least that was how Percy described it. He routinely swallowed Goody's Powders, two at a time, and washed them down with a Coca-Cola. He must have had a lot of pain or something. He liked to give me the "hot head." He would hold me down and rub his fist quickly over the top of my head. It burned and made me mad. I squirmed to get away. He thought it was funny.

"One day, them boys won't be boys no more and it will be your ass, Joel," Percy warned, but Joel paid him no mind.

"That day will never come when them boys can do anything with me," he replied.

During the summer, Joel enjoyed sitting on the long white wooden bench in front of the store and listening to the NASCAR races. He was a stubborn defender of Darrell Waltrip. It usually came down to Richard Petty, Cale Yarborough, or Darrell Waltrip. All the old men had their favorites and laid down bets on who would win. Most of the time the bet was a dollar. From time to time, Percy would get fed up with some of their big talk and would throw down a hundred-dollar bill and say, "Now put up or shut up." That normally took care of that because none of them had a hundred dollars to their name.

John D. was the "Tractor Man." He was gruff, mostly quiet, and a bit reserved in his manners. He was a medium-built man always with a couple days' growth of graying beard. His face was hard and aging, and his teeth didn't look too good from the yellow tobacco stains. He walked with a slight limp. He usually wore work pants and a flannel shirt, even in the summer. He slept in a room in the back of the store. Percy let him sleep there free to help protect the store from break-ins. He kept a shotgun in the back of the store, and Percy told him, "If you catch some son of a bitch breaking into my store, wait till he's in and kill the hell out of him. I'll take care of you."

John D. had been an Army soldier and had gotten shot in the buttocks during World War II. At least that's what they always said. He drove the tractors and kept the fields plowed and disked. He limped around the store and did light work on the farm equipment.

Argo was the "Sweeper" and known as the oldest black man alive. He was very skinny and always wore overalls. His face was sunken and marred with deep lines of experience and hardship. Argo also walked with a limp. He hobbled around with a broom in hand and kept the store and parking lot swept up. Percy said that Argo was so damn old that Argo knew people who were old when Percy was a young boy. They guessed him to be well over a hundred when he finally died.

Argo didn't seem to like people around him. If I got too close, he would swoosh the broom at me and mumble a few words. He mumbled and muttered all the time when he worked, and I didn't understand him. He could recall the names of people and families who'd lived around there for generations. He could recollect people's entire family tree. If a person entered the store who Argo had met fifteen years earlier, and only once, he could recall the person's name. Most people thought he made it all up, but the old timers said he was right on the mark and knew what he was talking about. Argo said he could remember when Percy's daddy, Ole Man Josh, used to hop little Percy on his knee when he was just a little boy. Percy said it was the damnedest thing he had ever seen. Reflecting back on Argo, it's possible that he must have been some misunderstood genius. Argo lived with a local tobacco farmer named OC who took care of Argo and gave him room and board.

Howard, or "Reno," was one of the whiskey men. Nobody called him the "Whiskey Man," but everybody knew he was. When I knew him, Reno was an old black man, with a deep baritone voice. He was really not old at all—maybe forty-nine or fifty—it just seemed that way to me. He smiled a lot. He had an egg-sized knot on the front of his forehead that never went away. He wore pantyhose on his hair sometimes. His voice was very deep and clear. His back was straight and strong. In the summer he always cut the toes out of his shoes to "let his feet breathe." It just looked funny to me. I didn't know if his feet could really breathe or not. I wanted to cut mine out too, but Mama said she would whip me if I did. Other than Percy, Reno was my favorite because he would always play and tease with me.

Reno was my best friend. In fact, at the store, when I was just six years old, we actually nicknamed one another. One day, I was straddling a small whiskey barrel and holding a funnel that he was pouring whiskey into. He looked up and said, "Good job, Dino!"

"Thanks, Reno!" I shot right back.

That's how we got our nicknames. We also named my sister, Tammy, "Tamarina." Reno named Willis "Curry" and sometimes referred to him as "poorr, poorr ole Curry." He hung his head and looked at the ground when he spoke of "poorr ole Curry."

I considered Reno the seed of truth and fairness. He came from a time when truth and fairness were rare and one-sided when it came to white people dealing with Southern blacks. Reno kept an eye on the special parking spot at the end of the store. That was where people who wanted more than groceries parked. I'd watch Reno through the rear store windows as he serviced the customers with pints and half-gallons of whiskey. A half-gallon glass jar of whiskey was about as much as he would sell out the door. Both the pints and half-gallons were always covered in brown paper sacks. As he sat and waited for customers, me and Reno just hung out together around the store.

Cobb was the local sheriff. He was a large, robust man whose belly hung over his belt to the point of completely covering his belt buckle. He always wore a khaki-colored sheriff's uniform with his sheriff's badge on his chest. His belt and gun holster were made of brown pleated leather.

He kept a large wood-grip-handled revolver strapped in his holster. He would often take the pistol out, remove the bullets, and let me hold and point it. He constantly chewed on a cigar, and tobacco spit often drooled at the sides of his mouth from this habit. His lips were also stained from the cigar, as were his teeth. His head was large and his face seemed a bit square. His neck was huge and hung in several layers of fat. When he stood, it appeared his legs were molded together as one. His hands and fingers were thick and freckled. He wobbled slightly as he walked, the outside heels of his shoes worn considerably more than the insides. He talked with a bit of slur. All in all, Cobb was the spitting image of what people expected from a Southern sheriff, the kind who could deliver a line like "You're not from around here, are you, boy?" to a motorist he'd pulled over. Even though he visited the store often and talked with Percy and me, Percy was careful about what he said around him. After all, Cobb was a sheriff. The law was the law.

The store was the Flowers headquarters. Percy, Curry, Reno, Joel, and John D. were the only people there all the time for all the years that I was there. We were inside the operation. Of course, my sister, Tammy, and I were among the group as family. Everyone else was just regulars and customers. There were all types of people who came by and the store was alive with excitement most of the time. The store was where everyone went and where everything took place. It was the seat of Percy's empire and my paradise as a child.

The store was very large and was divided into eight or nine rooms. Two doors located at the center and front opened into the main entrance where all the customers came and went. Entering the door, a long L-shaped counter was to the left with a cash register manned by Curry. To the right, a wooden desk sat behind the counter. The counter top was lined with candy, all kinds and types of candy: candy cigarettes, bubble gum cigars, Mary Janes, Super Bubble, baseball cards wrapped with chewing gum, Baby Ruths, suckers, Hot Wheels car cards with gum—you name it. I was allowed to eat it at will. Behind the counter was a small area for special things like tape, alcohol, iodine, Band-Aids, men's hair combs, Vitalis hair tonic, cough syrup, and pocket knives. Along the front store window behind the counter were all types of motor oil like Wolf's Head and STP oil treatment.

Flowers Grocery Store sign

The dead flies were thick along the window counter where the oil was. Under the counter were brown paper sacks, dog collars, a 30-caliber short carbine, and a loaded shotgun and pistol. There was no need to call Sheriff Cobb until an issue was settled. Inside the door entry there was a rollable cigarette case, five shelves high with CAMEL across the top. Cigarettes of all brands filled the shelves. Back then most people smoked. The popular brands were Marlboro, Pall Mall, Lucky Strikes, and Camels. As a common customer courtesy, the store man always gave a pack of wooden matches to cigarette buyers.

Small things had their own importance—like the small record book where Percy noted store credits. Long before the days of credit cards, farm hands were allowed a certain amount of credit to buy drinks, groceries, and other items. As debtors paid their balances down, Curry marked the book and maintained the balances.

Near the back corner wall was an ice-cream freezer with all types of ice cream: ice cream sandwiches, Nutty Buddies, frozen ice, and Push-Ups. Orange Push-Ups were my favorite. Only problem was that in the hot summer heat they would always melt on my hands before I could eat them. Behind the ice cream freezer was a walk-in cooler where meats and some vegetables were kept. There were two drink boxes full of Coke, Pepsi, NuGrape, Orange Crush, Sun Drop, root beer, RC, Cheerwine, Tab, and my all-time favorite Mountain Dew. The right side of the store was lined with shelves that ran just about the length of the room. These shelves were stocked with pork and beans, potted meat, string beans, hog lard, and a lot of other kinds of foods, all that country folk would want. There were also a lot of dead flies on the cans and shelves.

At the back of the room were the many bags of dog food, fifty-pound bags stacked from the floor to near the ceiling. This was my favorite place to play. I climbed over the bags, walked on them, and could see over the entire store from the top of the stacks. In the center of the store were several big cushion chairs and several small wooden chairs with straw seats. The store crowd always sat at the store and watched the ball games on TV or listened to the car races on the radio. The men usually sat backwards in the wooden chairs and rested their arms on the chair backs. During the summer, the floor was covered with granulated green or red fly bait. It was fun to run and slide on. It sure killed a lot of flies, too. There were also flytraps that hung from the ceiling. The traps were curly, yellow, and sticky with flies stuck to them. I didn't like touching them.

To the right of the door entry was a fishing wall where all the fishing lures and cane poles hung. People could buy whatever they needed to fish in the seven local ponds. Most people just used cane poles with fishing worms. Occasionally someone had a rod and reel but not usually. There was also a wooden box crank phone by the fishing wall. This was the first phone that I ever saw. It worked only between Percy's house and the store. It didn't ring too often, but his wife, Delma, sometimes called.

Delma was a beautiful black-haired woman. She spoke to me several times over the years, but I was not allowed to go over to the house when she was home. Mama said that Delma watched the store from her upstairs window.

The Flowers Home across
Highway 42 from the store, 1977

In the back of the store was storage. Crates of sodas and empty bottles were stacked taller than a man. A large wooden garage door also was at the back of the room where goods were moved in and out.

To the right were two other rooms. This was where John D., the Tractor Man, slept. It was a small room just large enough for a single bed. This part of the store was dark and looked scary. Through the store's main entrance and to the left end were a kitchen and Percy's office. The kitchen was where Reno, the Whiskey Man, did a lot of cooking. There were always huge black pots sitting on a massive black gas oven. Beside the oven was a vertical band saw for cutting shoulders and hams into slices. There were roaches there, too. Percy would sometimes tell Reno, "Clean that damn mess up back there." Percy said that he would never eat there, but he did often. Reno cooked gnat meat for my sister and me. At least he called it gnat meat. It was really hamburger. He baked an excellent pineapple cake, too. Reno also showed me how to cook sugar for coloring whiskey to red.

Percy's office adjoined the kitchen, and it was always interesting to me. In it was a large rollable steel safe several feet tall, several feet wide, and a couple of feet thick. Two large doors covered the front with a large dial wheel for the lock and a turn handle. Inside were several levels of shelving and on the side of the door were some tubes of tear gas to deter anyone who might try to break into the safe. Percy taught me the combination and I took pride in knowing it. I often opened the door and carefully inspected the vials of tear gas located on the door behind the combination spinner. A bathroom was next to the office and there was a small room behind the bathroom whose door was always locked. The very end of the store had once been a restaurant but now served as a storage area for chicken feed, a set of long steel rollers, and other stuff, including a small yellow go-cart.

The outside of the store, in front, was for parking and had three gas pumps. The regular gas pumps were red and the Hi-Test pump was white. The center red pump was older and required a crank handle to be rotated several times to zero out the price numbers. Curry usually served as the gas attendant.

The tractors were parked at the end of the store lot. There was a yellow Cub Cadet that stayed under the awning at the end of the store sidewalk. Reno's car, a Massey Ferguson 135, and a Massey Ferguson 1100 sat there too. There was also a large two-story barn at the end of the store. Bulls, horses, chickens, and farm implements were in the barn. Men sometimes came by just to sit and talk. I knew most of the regulars by name by the time I was ten.

I received an informal but valuable education at that store. I even learned some cuss words and also learned when not to say them. I would say them to myself sometimes just to see what they sounded like. Son of a bitch, hell fire, crazy nigger, good-god-ah-mighty, and hotta mighty no. I picked up a lot of learning there. I could even start a car by myself. Back then, no one took the keys out of their vehicles, so sometimes I'd just start a truck and turn it off to see if I could do it.

While at the store, we saw all manner of people coming through, some of them not always pleasant. While I was pumping gas one Sunday afternoon, a car pulled up to the curb and a large black woman got out and went into the store. I walked in behind her and went behind the counter and stood beside Percy at the wooden desk. The lady purchased several sodas and a pack of cigarettes. Curry was working the cash register and rang up all of her items. The large woman asked for a book of matches in a Yankee accent. In his usual quiet, serious manner, Curry explained that he was out of matches.

The woman arrogantly responded, "What kinda joint is this, sells cigarettes and no matches? I want some matches." Percy and I watched as she flung her money onto the countertop. Before I knew what was happening, Percy leaped out of the desk chair and was standing in front of her with the shotgun pointed right in her face.

"You high-society black son of a bitch, ya take your New York ass out of here right now."

The woman ran out of the store and sprinted for her car as he followed her with the shotgun. I could see her running to her car through the large store windowpanes. She was a sizable woman but a surprisingly fast runner and highly motivated. As she sprinted to the car, the car doors flew open. Three men helped her clamber in as they sped away. I knew that Percy's shotgun was loaded at that moment, and watching from the window, I was certain he would have shot her if she had said one more thing to him. There was no excuse for bad manners, it seemed.

On the front sidewalk was a long white wooden bench. I called this "the bench of knowledge." Often Percy and I sat on the bench and watched people coming and going. Many times we just sat there and talked. We were sitting on the bench one day, and he sat with his elbows on his knees with his head held down. I was asking him to let me drive the dog truck or tractor, and he just looked over at me and smiled.

"Perry, I'd give ever' damn thang I own to be your age and feel as good as you do for just one day. You'll know one day that these are the best days of your life, right now while yer young. Hell, when you git to be my age you cain't do shit. But now you're full of piss and vinegar. Boy what I'd give to be young like you."

He didn't mince words even with me. Percy and I spent a lot of time together, and, for better or worse, he was my first role model.

It must have been around 1967 when I first took a glimpse of the unusual red car always parked at the southwest corner of the store's parking lot. I asked Percy to ride in it next time we went somewhere. It was summer and hot when he said, "Perry, c'mon, boy." It was time for me to go home and we were taking the red car. He picked me up and slid me through the windowless driver's side and I stepped over to the passenger seat. It was bare and stripped down inside. When the motor fired up, the car roared to life. The vibration came through the seat bottom. I was a little scared but mostly excited. He accelerated out of the parking lot going toward Archer Lodge and my house. As he said, "Hold on, Perry," I knew that something amazing was about to happen. He floored the gas pedal and the engine roared; that was my first lesson in acceleration. The speed built quickly and the wind rushed into the open car. I raised up and slightly stuck my head out the window to feel the wind push on my face. I felt his hand reach over and hold onto me. When I opened my mouth, the wind pushed it wide, blowing my jaws open. That must have been how it felt to the hounds when they held their heads in the wind outside of a car window. Then I held my hand out to feel the wind push against it. The little red car roared down the road faster than I had ever been. It was a thrill.

When we reached the dirt path that led down to my house, Percy whipped the car onto the road and again pressed hard on the gas pedal. The engine roared, and the car fishtailed down the path. Percy never let up and just said, "Hotta mighty no," and smiled as he held onto his cigar in the corner of his mouth. He saw the thrill on my face as I smiled back. As we blasted down the road we hit several potholes, which made the car feel light and loose. I looked back to see the large dust trail following us. When we slowed down, a mighty cloud engulfed the car, and we were covered with dust. Percy was wearing his usual dress pants and white dress shirt with cigar holes in it and his usual hush puppies. He didn't seem to mind that he was covered in dust. We must have surprised the dogs and arrived before they could run up the road to meet us. My little soul was filled with joy. In one day, I had discovered acceleration, tire spin, fish tail, and sheer excitement in the little red Studebaker Golden Hawk. I never was sure why they called it the Golden Hawk, as it was all red.

One spring day in 1970, Percy and I sat on the bench of knowledge. I was telling Percy about all the toys that Santa Claus had brought for my friends Scotty and Dean. Scotty was Percy's brother's grandson who lived just across the woods. His father, Billy, was the Grand Dragon of the Johnston County Ku Klux Klan klavern, and he seemed very well off. Scotty and I were only two months apart in age and played together regularly. His mama and my mama knew each other and had been pregnant at the same time.

Santa had brought Scotty a motorcycle, helmet, new gun, and a lot of other toys. That year Santa had only brought me a plastic sword and the same ole candy in my stocking as the last few years. I was mad that Santa hadn't brought me more.

Percy said, "Santa Claus didn't bring them boys all that stuff, Perry. Their daddy bought all them toys for them children. Now don't you worry. If I bought all that shit for you, then you wouldn't be worth a shit when you grow up." This didn't change the way I felt, and he could see that I was still sad. Sometime later that same day, he called for me to come and go with him.

"Where we going?" I asked.

"Just come on, Perry. We going to Clayton."

We climbed into the big Cadillac and roared out of the store parking lot onto Highway 42. In a few minutes, we were on Main Street and walking into Western Auto. As we walked into the store, Percy stopped only about five steps into the door entry. He pointed to a black mini-bike sitting on the floor. It had a tag hanging from the handlebars.

"You thank you can ride that, Perry?" he asked.

He bought the mini-bike and loaded it into the Cadillac trunk. Guess I was on my way to not being worth a shit, but it sure felt good and it helped me forget about Santa Claus.

Over the next ten years, I spent a lot of time with Percy at the store up until his death. When he went somewhere, I went with him. That's just how it was. His earlier years in the moonshining business had kept him very busy and robbed him of family time. Mama said that in the 1950s Percy was gone all the time. Lucky for me and Tammy those busy years had mostly passed, so we had the chance to see him often and he enjoyed the time with us. The store was much more than his brain center for moonshining operations. It was a safe haven for me as a child, a place where I found complete confidence in myself. It was an education, the place where I learned about people and life. Every child should have that kind of place,

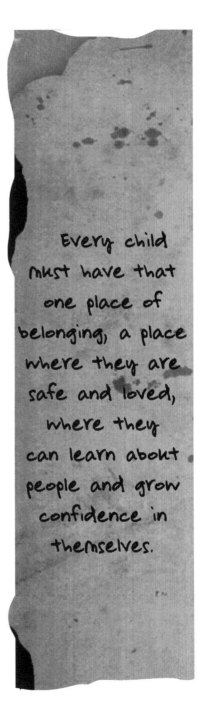

Every child must have that one place of belonging, a place where they are safe and loved, where they can learn about people and grow confidence in themselves.

a place where they truly belong, where they are safe and loved. For me, that place was the Flowers Store. Even with my childhood of secrets and hardship, I consider myself fortunate to have had such a place.

Perry Sullivan and Percy Flowers at the Flowers Store in Clayton, NC, in 1978

The old barn beside the store where whiskey barrels were kept

4

THE BENCH
OF KNOWLEDGE

Dear Josh and John,

The wooden, white-painted bench that sat at the front of Percy's store had been there forever and was the centerpiece of the store's entryway. The men sat here to listen to the NASCAR races and baseball games on the radio. I called it "the bench of knowledge" because Percy and I had many father-to-son talks there. I never thought then that I would ever think of that bench this many years down the road. That bench is where I first heard the story of Percy Jr. and the ill-fated flight. Here is where we sat and talked to Sheriff Cobb and I wondered why he slurred his words. It is where Joel, the Dog Man, gave me the "hot head" and Percy warned him to stop or else. I sat on that bench so very many Sundays to watch for cars to pull up to the tanks so that I could rush out to pump the gas into people's cars. This was the same bench where Reno and I sat and watched for those special customers who pulled to the end of the store to buy whiskey. I heard quite a few stories on the bench of knowledge. So let me tell you a few.

Best Not Let the Dog Out

Percy and I were sitting on the old bench watching the cars come and go. We'd just opened a small Coca-Cola and poured a pack of salted peanuts into the bottle. Peanuts in a bottle of Coke or Pepsi made a really good snack. An older model truck pulled up and parked in front of the store. A middle-aged man opened the door and stepped out as his black and white husky dog rushed to the window of the truck to watch his master go into the store. Percy pointed to the truck.

"Them type of dogs will chase and kill anything, Perry," he said.

The man was in the store for a few minutes and then came out with some fishing worms and a soda. He was looking back over his shoulder and called out to Percy.

"I'll try that pond across the street," he said, referring to fishing in the nearby pond.

"Hey, you about to go fishing over there?" Percy called back.

"Yeah, I'm going to try it and see if they'll bite," the man said.

"Well, OK, but make sure you don't let that dog out," Percy warned. "I have some chickens over there and that dog'll kill 'em."

The man reassured Percy that he would keep the dog in the truck and not let him out. He climbed back into his truck, backed up, and drove across Highway 42 to park. With a clear line of sight from the store, we watched from the bench. He gathered his fishing gear from the back of the truck and then walked around to the front to let the husky out. The dog was no sooner out of the truck than he gave chase after a hen, with biddies, and killed the chicken by clamping it in its teeth and shaking it. The dog immediately took chase after another chicken and did the same. The man just stood by the truck and yelled for the dog to return, but the dog ignored him and kept chasing the chickens.

Percy leaped from the bench and ran inside the store.

"C'mon, Howard. Go with me!" he yelled to Reno.

Percy came from the store toting a Remington pump shotgun.

"C'mon, Perry. Go with me. Dat dam' dog is killing my chickens over there."

We jumped into his silver Dodge truck. He threw the loaded shotgun between us and rushed across the highway to where the man and truck were. As we got out, I saw Reno running from the store to join us. Percy exited the truck and hollered at the man.

"Catch that dog before he kills all my chickens!" he told him.

The man dashed toward his dog after Percy gave the warning, but it was too late—the dog had killed several chickens and Percy had the gun drawn onto the dog to shoot.

"Don't you shoot my dog!" the man called out roughly.

Percy then pointed the gun directly at the fisherman as he walked even closer.

"I told you to keep that dog in the truck and not let him out. Now he's killed my chickens. You get your ass out of here right now, you son of a bitch."

The man started to move toward the driver's side of his truck and Percy more emphatically pointed the shotgun at him.

"You better stop right there. If you put your hand inside that damn truck, I'm going to kill you. I mean stop. Now, move your ass away from that door before I have to kill you," Percy said, all business.

The man took a couple of steps away. By then Reno was standing beside me.

"Howard," Percy said. "Hold this gun on him, and if he moves, shoot him. He has a damn gun or knife in that truck." Percy had keen instincts.

As Howard held the shotgun on the man, Percy moved quickly to the driver's side door, opened it, and searched the truck. I could see him through the truck window opening the glove compartment. Percy turned around holding a Bowie knife about a foot long. He held it up.

"I tole you he had sumthin' in that truck," he said. Holding the big knife, Percy walked toward us. "Perry, let's go. Howard, keep the gun on him until he gets his ass out of here and if he tries something, kill him."

Percy and I returned to the store as Reno escorted the man off the premises. Child that I was, I was just relieved it was all over.

If You Shoot Percy, Then You Better Kill Him

It was just another day of fun at the store as we sat on the bench of knowledge. Percy sat on my right side and Reno on my left. They were just sitting quietly, doing nothing in particular, but I was a curious chatterbox as usual.

"Hey, Percy, tell me something," I said.

"What you want to know, Perry?"

"I don't know," I replied. "Just tell me a story."

"Perry, you sure are full of questions, boy." He smiled.

Reno chimed in. "What ever happened to dat man that shot at you?"

"Oh, yeah. Well, Perry, I got shot one time, he like to got me."

"What happened?"

"Well, this man pulled up where I was and got out with a shotgun and just shot me. He shot two times. I dove into my Cadillac where I had that thirty-eight laying on the seat. I came out firing, but he got away. I walked to the back of my Cadillac and put my foot on the bumper, and the blood just runned down my leg and dripped all over the bumper and ground."

I was fascinated. "What happened to him? Did you get him?"

"Well, Perry, the funniest thang happened," he said. "That man that shot me was in a bar and a man just happened to walk up to him, place a pistol in his chest, and shot him. Yea, it just wahn't his day. But he never shot at nobody else."

It never paid to threaten or assault Percy without finishing the job.

Brother against Brother

The bench was full of knowledge and wisdom. While I pushed for stories and conversation, Percy occasionally seemed to want to pass on advice.

One day Percy and I sat on the bench as I ate an Orange Push-Up.

"Perry, you need to be careful about people. A man was about to send me up," he said, apparently referring to someone testifying in court and sending Percy to prison.

"Huh?"

"You just can't trust people," he said. "It was sad, but that boy killed his brother."

"What for?" I asked.

"Well, his brother—who was killed—worked for me and was going to talk to the Man when his brother found out and killed him to protect me," he said.

I didn't really know what to make of that. I just turned and finished my ice cream as Percy seemed a little sad.

The Apple Doesn't Fall Far

It was about 1971. Percy had taught me, right there on that bench, how to take care of myself. I was telling him about a bully who had been picking on me on the bus ride to school. The bully kept thumping my ears. It was winter and this really hurt since my ears were so cold. The bully was an upperclassman, much larger than I was, and I was just in the fourth grade. I told Percy about the ear thumping and how the bully had bonked me and other kids on the head with his class ring.

"Now, Perry, don't take no shit from nobody or they will run all over you," he said. "You have to stand up for yourself."

"But he's a lot bigger than me."

"Well, lookah here," he said. "A big-ass man jumped on me one time and he was beating me in my face so hard he didn't know I was gittin' my pocket knife out. When I got it open, I started dragging it across his big ass as hard as I could. You never seen a man move so fast."

"OK," I said, considering this.

A few days later on the bus, the bully bonked me as usual on the head as he sat down with me. I noticed as he sat that he rested his right hand on his school book. I cautiously opened my three-ring binder and unzipped my pencil holder. I removed a very large-sized, freshly sharpened pencil. This pencil was the width of three standard number two pencils put together. I gently slipped the pencil by my side and waited as he thumped the kid's ear in front of us. He laughed as the younger child grabbed his ear in pain. The bully again placed his hand on the book he was holding. I took the large pencil in both hands and with all my might drove it into the top of his hand resting on the book. The pencil lead broke off completely in his hand, and blood began to run out. He started yelling and quickly moved to another seat while dropping his books onto the floor. Even though he was bigger than all of us, I pointed my pencil at him and gave him a stern warning.

"You better not thump my dam ears no more and I mean it," I told him.

This turned out to be a well-learned lesson for him as he never thumped my ears again. He never sat with me again either.

Percy's advice had proved true.

"You Just Won't Leave It Alone, Perry"

I used to badger Percy to teach me how to make moonshine, and he resisted for a long while.

"Percy, why won't you show me how?" I would pester him. But Percy had bigger dreams for me involving veterinary medicine.

"Now, Perry, you need to forget about it and let me send you to veterinarian school," he said. "Boy, you will have licenses to steal. I'll set you up right here and you can take care of my hounds. You know that vet in Smithfield charged me a fortune for that dog we carried down there last week."

We had carried to the vet a dog that had gotten tangled in barbed wire fencing during our hunt the week before. Percy and I waited and watched as the vet stitched the open and ragged wound. It looked pretty bad to me, and there was a lot of blood. In fact, it didn't seem like something I wanted to do from what I saw that day.

"Perry, them days of whiskey making are gone," Percy said, shaking his head. "You can't make no money no more and you can't trust no one. Use to be, a dollar meant something and you could trust people. Today the government has so many informants that you just can't do it no more. And if you get caught it'uh ruin you. You don't need to mess with it, but you just won't leave it alone."

Parents want the best for their children, but do the children listen? No....

Birdshot for Thieves

"Howard, you 'member that ole army boy that came by here with a flat tire?" Percy asked Reno one day as we sat on the bench.

"Oh yeah. I shaw do, that I do," said Reno. "Perry, an army man came by here during the war," he said, referring to World War II.

"He had a flat tire on his car. I told the man I'd be glad to fix it for him. I gave him a free tire and had the tire man put it on for him. But then the tire man came up and said he couldn't find his jack and tire wrench. So I walked down there and asked the fellow to open his trunk to see if the missin' jack and tire wrench was in the trunk.

"He'd snatched the tools and put 'em in his trunk after we fixed his tire. I grabbed the shotgun and he took off running across the parking lot. I had birdshot in that gun so when I fired at him, I never seen so much dust fly outta ah coat. When them shot hit the back of his coat, dust just flew out.

"Next day the doctor came by and said what happened to him. He said that he picked more shot out of that man's back that he ever had seen. Said he picked them out until he got tired of picking and quit. Bet he didn't steal no more tools from people."

No Means No

Percy and I were sitting on the bench one day and I was completely bored. I walked to the end of the store where the yellow Cub tractor sat on the sidewalk. It was the one the Dog Man used to cut the grass in the dog lots. I climbed aboard and pretended to drive and shift the gears, making tractor noises as if I was driving. Percy saw me shifting the gears over and over.

"Perry, stop messing with those gears before you break that thang," he hollered down at me.

I heard him, looked right at him, and then continued to pretend to drive and shift.

He swiftly got up and joined me at the tractor to administer a spanking.

"Now when I say no, I mean no," he told me afterward. "Now don't mess with them gears no more."

That was the only spanking Percy ever gave me. He must have felt badly about it as he offered me a Mountain Dew a short time later.

A Rare Sight to See

It was very rare to see Percy with a perplexed look on his face, but I knew how to make it happen. We were sitting on the bench one day. Percy was chewing his cigar and spitting across the sidewalk onto the parking lot. I was out of options for fun.

"Whose boy are you, Perry?" he had asked me many times. This was a tender ritual between us, for, indeed, we both knew I was Percy's son.

This one day, however, I decided to get a reaction. I mischievously leaned over against Percy and whispered in his ear, "I'm going to go tell Curry whose boy I am."

Percy was stupefied. "Shhhh, Perry. You better be quiet."

"I'm going to tell him," I said a bit louder with a smile.

Percy just sat there with a perplexed look on his face. He wasn't quite sure how to respond.

"I'm just playing with you," I smiled, chuckling.

He mouthed the words, "You better not." He rested his elbows on his knees and placed his face in his hands with a faint smile.

5

COCKFIGHTING

Dear Josh and John,

Today, cockfighting is something you can only read about or maybe hear about on the news. But it did take place and people from all walks of life attended. In recent years, cockfighting has been portrayed as just a bunch of backwoods folks getting together for a backyard chicken fight. Back in the day, however, cockfighting was popular, and men from all over the country came from far and wide for the events. Percy was well known for his fast Reds and powerful, hard-hitting Grey fighting cocks. Over the years he had perfected the bloodline for stamina and strength. Let me tell you how it worked...

Silver spurs slashed through the air, ripping feathers and flesh as the gamecocks flew into the air and fought to their death. This event wasn't for the fainthearted nor for the tender sensibilities of animal rights activists. Cockfighting was a sport—if you could call it a sport—that folks from all walks of life came from far and wide to attend. There were low-lifes, thieves, murderers, business- and money-men crowding the smoke-filled cock-fighting arena. They all loved the action and the opportunity to make a fast dollar by betting on their favorite feathered warriors.

One day at the store, Reno was fixing some breakfast in the store kitchen. Eddie, the chicken handler, sipped away at a cup of dark black coffee. Black coffee was the norm. Back then there weren't any Starbucks or other gourmet sissified coffee shops. Words like "latte" and "venti" sounded effeminate enough to have been fightin' words. Maxwell House in a metal number ten steel can was the one and only coffee. And folks never threw out the empty cans because they could be put to many other practical uses, for example, as savings jars, fishing worm holders, nut and bolt keepers, and even spittoons.

Percy stood by the vertical band saw as he discussed the upcoming cockfight with Reno and Eddie. "Eddie, which ones are ready? Do you think that ole Grey is good? We need to pick the ones to take 'cause the fight's next week in Virginia."

"They all be looking good and sparring fine," Eddie said. "The ole Grey seems ready and dat damn Red can hit like you never seen."

"Well, you work 'em and early next week let's decide and then let 'em rest the day before we go," advised Percy.

Fighting cocks, Greys and Reds,
wander about their shelters
(Note the rooster's heel tether)

Reno finished cooking breakfast and put the bacon and eggs on paper plates along with biscuits and Karo syrup. The grease from the bacon and eggs soaked through the doubled white paper plates and made them flimsy to hold. We sat at the table and ate the breakfast, talking and planning out the upcoming cockfight. Anticipation was high.

"Now, Eddie, you going to take the station wagon, and me and Perry are riding with Billy," Percy told Eddie.

There were several breeds of fighting cocks favored by breeders and handlers: Reds, Greys, Speckles, and a few others. Percy preferred to breed only Reds and Greys. Reds were fast, while Greys were hard-hitting and more powerful. The Reds had deep dark red/orange feathers with long, dark tail feathers. The Greys had yellowish white necks with black bodies and tail feathers. Both were slim and muscular. These birds were deadly, able to drive their spurs into their targets with pinpoint accuracy. If the handler became the least bit careless, he could expect a deep, painful stabbing puncture from a spur. The roosters were bred to fight and were 100 percent "game." They had to be separated and physically restrained from one another at all times to prevent unwanted fights that could injure them.

Percy bred the Reds and Greys in rows of triangular, wooden shelters on about six acres of land. Many of them were heel tethered to prevent escape, and each was hand fed a snuffbox full of corn or seed every day.

Across from the store was Percy's house and behind his house was a small garage. His son, Percy Jr., once kept his new black Cadillac parked under this garage. One day, a gamecock escaped from a pen and walked into the garage.

The cock saw his reflection in the shiny black Cadillac and began to attack the image. He fought so hard that he scratched and scarred the Cadillac's fender. Percy said that Percy Jr. was so mad he'd just about cried. Well, that just goes to show how "game" fighting cocks are, but smart they certainly are not.

We had moved to a house on Motorcycle Road when I was six years old so that the bus could pick my sister and me up for school. It was six miles to school. Behind the house was the fighting training room and sparring area where Eddie trained the roosters. Just behind the training building was a clear, flat patch of grass that made for a good sparring area. Percy and Eddie were inside looking over the roosters as I listened quietly.

"Eddie, grab that Red right there and take him outside. I'll take this Grey and let's see how they look together," Percy said.

They took the cocks, one at a time, and placed them on the walking bench. Percy held the rooster as Eddie laced a pair of miniature boxing gloves onto the cock's spurs.

Percy leaned over to me. "Here, Perry. Hold this rooster while we get the other one. "Now be careful with him and hold him right up against your side like that," he told me, as he placed the high-spirited rooster in my arms and pressed him against my side. I could see the rooster looking around and was doing all I could not to upset him or let him get away.

"Perry, take him outside and I'll be there in a minute when we get this one ready." I carefully walked out the door and down the two cinderblock steps to a sparring area under two trees.

In just a couple of minutes, Percy came out and carefully took the rooster out of my arms and smiled. "Now, Perry, that's a real fighting cock you have there."

Eddie came out of the training room and stepped down the block steps holding a Grey. He kept the rooster's head covered under his elbow so that the two couldn't see one another. Percy and Eddie faced one another about ten feet apart, walked up face to face, and let the roosters look and peck away. Then they stepped back and pitched the roosters together. The two roosters ran toward one another at full force, head on. They met and flew straight up while fighting. I heard the thump as they collided just prior to flying up together. It was beastly and beautiful. They fell to the ground tangled like two wrestlers on a gym floor. Feathers flew as they rolled on the ground together and then again flew up to fight.

Percy yelled out, "Hotta mighty no, dem son of bitches can go!"

Eddie stepped in and separated the two cocks. The fighting cocks panted hard like runners who'd just finished a marathon. Still they tried to reach one another to fight. The leather boxing gloves had saved their lives. That would not have been the case in the real fight where they would wear the steel spurs or swords.

Eddie came by in the early morning and loaded eight fighting cocks into brown vented boxes and placed them into the back of the station wagon. The station wagon was used just for transporting the cocks to the fights. It had air conditioning to keep them cool on the long ride to Virginia. We would be riding in the car with Billy. Mama got up early and cooked some fatback biscuits for us to take on the trip.

She cautioned me, "Perry, you be careful at that place and watch out for people. Dares some bad people at them kinda places."

I helped wrap the fatback biscuits in aluminum foil and put them in a brown paper sack. A silver Cadillac pulled up into the driveway and Mama and I went out to meet it. Billy and another man sat in the front seats and I got into the back with Percy. Mama walked up to the car and told Percy that he'd better take care of me. We said our good-byes and Billy pulled the shiny Cadillac onto the red clay dirt path and we went on our way to Virginia. Percy had a cooler full of small Coca-Colas.

"Damn, what's that smelling so good?" Billy asked.

I opened the sack and handed out the fatback biscuits while Percy opened the Coca-Colas and passed them out. We rode for several hours to get to the cockfight. The men liked smoking cigars. The inside of the car was so filled with cigar smoke that I could fan it with my hands and see it swirl. There was always a cloud of smoke in the car, even with the window cracked. The men would tap their ashes out the windows or into a cup. Quite often the ashes fell onto their shirts, leaving burn marks like the ones Percy always had on the front of his shirts. Even today, the smell of cigar smoke reminds me of riding in Percy's truck.

After several hours of driving, we arrived in Virginia and the asphalt road became a dirt path. We pulled onto the path and followed the curves for about half a mile until we came up to a large barn in the middle of the woods with many cars and trucks parked outside. We saw our station wagon and knew that Eddie had made it OK. Billy parked the Cadillac alongside the other vehicles. As we exited the Cadillac, Percy reached down and picked up his hammer-less .38 Smith & Wesson detective revolver that had been lying on the seat and placed it in his pants pocket. As we walked up to the barn, he told us about a time he went to a cockfight and everyone there got robbed at gunpoint. He said men with shotguns made everybody stand in the middle of the ring, empty their pockets, and then strip down to their underpants. The robbers then took the money and fled. I didn't want to get robbed, so I stayed near Percy.

We entered the large barn and it was chock full of people. In the center of the barn was a large dirt circle about twenty-five to thirty feet in diameter called the "pit" surrounded by three-foot-high wire. Bleachers encircled the entire pit with the exception of several walk-through areas. The ceilings were high, probably twenty-five or more feet tall. Behind the bleachers were two drag pits—small, fenced eight-by-ten-feet areas—in front of a chopping block that was used for beheading the roosters after the fight. This was where the main pit fights were moved when the roosters began to tire to the point that they had to be revived in order to continue fighting.

Percy and I were in the holding area where Eddie had placed the roosters in individual pens. "Eddie, watch out for these sons a bitches. Don't let 'em steal any of these roosters," Percy cautioned him.

Eddie assured him that they would be fine. I could hear some yelling coming from the main pit as Percy and I made our way back to the bleachers. We worked our way up to find a seat beside Billy to watch the fights. The pit boss was the referee and announced the first set of cocks to fight. Each handler showed his rooster to the audience and then allowed a man to weigh the rooster on a set of scales. The pit boss directed each handler to a side of the pit ring and then made the motion for them to approach one another. As the handlers faced off in the middle of the ring, they allowed the fighting cocks to look one another in the eye and take a few practice pecks, just the way Percy and Eddie had done behind the training area. This time the cocks were armed with deadly two- or three-inch spurs. The spurs were the diameter of the inside of a writing pen, slightly curved and tapered to a needle-sharp point. They were precision-made weapons attached to a deadly fighting machine.

As the fight was about to begin, Percy whispered to Billy, "Look sitting over there. He ain't s'pose to even be in the country. He was extradited for what he done."

I asked Percy who he was talking about, and he made a small pointing motion across the pit and said, "That big fat man over there with the gray coat on and the silver hair."

We were interrupted when the pit boss gave the sign to fight. The two handlers stepped back and released the mighty fighting warriors. They performed just as they had during the practice sparring, running full speed toward one another to meet with a resounding clash. The two flew vertically, entwined in a ferocious embrace as their bodies tumbled down to the pit floor. They fought and struggled until their spurs seemed locked and neither could stand. The pit boss motioned for the handlers to separate the cocks. The handlers separated them just enough to allow them to spring back together and fight again. This went on for several minutes. The crowd hollered for their favorite to win. As they yelled, they made hand gestures across the pit to one another in the sign language of pit betting, making bets and laying odds.

As they tired, the cocks were slowing down in their attacks. The pit boss directed the handlers to move the fight to the drag pit. As the handlers moved to the drag pit, the bettors moved along with them. The handlers were miracle workers reviving the roosters with their own mouths as the bettors looked on. The cocks fought to the death. Then the pit boss announced the winner and the bettors collected their winnings.

Both drag pits were full with cocks fighting to the bitter end when I heard the pit boss call Percy Flowers. Eddie entered the ring with a broad-chested Grey.

*Broad-chested
Grey fighting cock, 1978*

The crowd recognized Percy Flowers's name; obviously his reputation for a finely tuned bloodline preceded him. The crowd was betting before the fight even began.

Percy leaned over to me and asked, "Perry, you have any money?"

Of course he knew that a ten-year-old didn't have any money. He handed me a hundred-dollar bill and said, "You can keep it or bet it, your choice."

I thought for a moment and knew that his rooster was a favorite. I waved my hand and yelled, "Twenty on the Grey!"

A man just a few rows down looked at me and motioned with his hand that he would take the bet.

Percy saw the transaction and smiled. "Now keep an eye on him so at the end you can settle up," he told me.

Eddie and the other handler received the pit boss's signal to start the fight. The two roosters left the handlers' hands like thoroughbred racehorses out of the gates. The crowd cheered as the cocks twirled high into the air and came down fighting. They fought until they too were ready for the drag pit. I hurried down the bleachers looking back at Percy as he followed, slightly afraid to be separated from him with the entire crowd around me. Making my way to one of the two pits, I saw the axe man swing the axe and decapitate a rooster. This stopped me in my tracks for a moment. Then I saw Eddie enter the drag pit with the battered warrior.

The two handlers released the cocks as they made a couple of hard hits at one another and then locked together lying on the ground, neither moving. Blood was oozing from the beak of the big Grey. The pit boss motioned and the handlers separated the roosters. Eddie placed his mouth over the big Grey's beak and head and sucked with all his might. He turned and spit the blood and mucous onto the ground. Then he placed his mouth back over the top of the rooster's head and blew his breath onto the top of the rooster's head. The big Grey indeed seemed as if a new breath of life had just entered his body. Eddie placed the big Grey down again and it hobbled toward the other cock that was itself barely standing. The Grey made a last slicing glance and then the two exhausted combatants fell together onto the ground, one on top of the other. The other cock was dead and the big Grey was nearly dead. The pit boss announced that the Flowers rooster was the winner. As Eddie picked up the rooster, I asked him whether the big Grey would be OK. He shook his head, and we took the bird to the chopping block. I asked him what he was doing, as if I didn't know.

Percy stepped up and said, "We have to cut their heads off when they are this bad off. They won't be able to fight again even if they live. We can't leave them alive cause somebody will take them and breed them for the bloodline."

I was sad to see the old Grey put to death after he had fought so fiercely to win. *Winning really ain't winning for the cocks.*

I collected my twenty dollars from the man that took my bet. Now I had $120! Throughout the night I watched and betted. At one point I had over $300. It was the sixth fight for our cocks and so far we had done well. Eddie brought out another big-chested Grey as the crowd cheered. He was fighting another well-known breeder's line. I was sure to win, so I bet all I had, knowing that this amount would double. If I won I would have over $600—not bad for one night's work for a young boy!

Once again, the pit boss motioned to fight. Eddie released our best fighting Grey. The two cocks flew straight up and fell to the pit floor. The big Grey just lay there as the other rooster tried to walk. It seemed that the big Grey's head was stuck to the other cock's spur. The big Grey took a direct head shot during the fly up and was killed instantly. The other cock's spur stuck completely through his head and was fixed there. I was shocked and wondered if I really had to pay that much money over a head shot. The other punter came directly over to me to collect. I paid him all I had. For the rest of the night, I was too upset about losing the money to pay attention to the fights. When we left, Percy asked me how much I had won. I explained the head shot loss.

"Perry, I once lost ten thousand dollars in less than five seconds on Samson. Samson was a prize fighter who lost the same way. But here is what I want you to learn. Don't ever bet on outcomes you can't predict, especially if you can't afford to lose. Let that be a lesson." I have never bet since that day, nor do I have a desire to.

Percy had taught me a priceless life lesson. The lesson was clear but hard to accept. Some may think that a cockfighting arena was no place for a boy. The man with the gray coat had been indicted for fixing horse races. All types of folks were there. Businessmen, thieves, drunks, preachers, and councilmen. My sons often ask me how I can so easily talk with and make friends with anyone. I believe this ability comes from those early days when I had the opportunity to mix with many different types of people on even terms. I experienced poverty at its worst and sat at the store among the elite. The point is, I hope my children will always be considerate to everyone they meet. You can learn something from every person you encounter. Choose your words and actions carefully and make every interaction a "win-win" situation.

Also, just as important, don't gamble if you can't afford to lose.

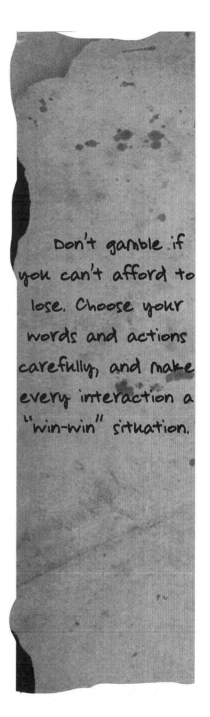

Don't gamble if you can't afford to lose. Choose your words and actions carefully, and make every interaction a "win-win" situation.

6

THE FOX RACE

Dear Josh and John,

Did you know that foxhounds can sing? They sure can. To many of the old timers, there was no better music than the sound of thirty or forty foxhounds baying in unison while chasing the hot scent of a sly wild fox. The hounds were trained from pups and their nature was hardwired through their bloodline. Mixing bloodlines to get the perfect hound was more than just science, it was art. Percy earned a reputation as the master of manipulating bloodlines to create unyielding stamina and drive. His foxhounds were favorites among hunters, and the price to own one was steep.

As a boy I often went with Percy to listen to the foxhounds hunt across the open uninhabited forest and fields. Josh and John, let me take you back to a typical foxhunt as I remember it as a boy.

Besides cockfighting, Percy lived for foxhound racing. He says he was just a young boy when his father, Ole Man Josh, introduced him to the sport. It was his love as a young boy, and as an adult, this passion served as his outlet from the strenuous demands of running a moonshining empire. Percy's reputation as a master breeder came from his strict and pure bloodlines that he'd perfected over his lifetime. As a devoted practitioner of the breeding art, he knew the right breeding techniques and combinations for bringing out desirable traits. In an article entitled "Thrills Without Kills," *The Tarheel* quoted Percy as stating, "I guess I've thrown away more good money trying to breed hounds than any man alive."

In 1946, Coy, a dog he sold, won the first US Open for foxhound racing. Again in 1948, Cry Baby Cry, another of Percy's hounds, captured the third US Open. The article further stated, "Throughout the past few decades, his hounds placed consistently in the national competitions, but Flowers' greatest thrill came in the late 1960's when, out of a field of two hundred in the U.S. Open, his hounds placed first, third and fifth."

Percy Flowers with one of his prized
foxhounds from the Tenth HGA
US Open Annual Field Trials

Percy Flowers with another prized hound

Other hunters guessed at the breeds' bloodlines and tried to duplicate these traits for successful hounds. Among hound breeders, it was common knowledge that Percy had perfected an elite and never-before-accomplished blend of unmatched stamina and "drive." His hounds were so driven that some would run to the point of ruining their legs if they weren't stopped early enough. Some were difficult to catch and load after a hunt and would run for several days until completely exhausted. People would pay thousands of dollars just to own one such creature—that is, if they could buy one for any price. Percy was known as a tough man to deal with when it came to buying a foxhound. According to *The Tarheel*: "Those who have done business with him will vow that he is one of the hardest men in the world to buy a hound from...There are some hounds, he claims, that he just cannot put a price on. And why should he, he argues—'If you have what you consider to be the best, why compete against yourself?'"

Percy's foxhound breeding stock was so good that thieves routinely attempted to steal them to acquire the bloodline. Dogs often went missing during hunts and rumors swirled that someone had stolen them. All of the hounds wore leather collars with brass plates bearing their names. I helped stamp the names on the brass plates and punch holes in the leather collars.

Percy had over 200 hounds and several customized trucks with special steel cages to carry them to the hunt. The largest truck was a green Ford with a granny gear and a double-decker cage on it. We could load twenty dogs onto it and often did. I liked the double-decker best because I could clearly see the dogs in the upper level when I stood outside the truck.

Once my sister and I rode from the store to our home in the dog cage. We ate ice cream push-ups as we bounced down the dirt road in the back of the truck cage. Even though the dust from the road enveloped the cage and filled our lungs, we laughed all the way. The other truck, Percy's personal truck, sported a single-decker cage. The tops of the cages were heavy duty, built strong enough for a person to stand on. We would often stand on top of the cage to better hear the race. Even the truck's bumpers were custom made, widened to about eighteen inches for easier loading and standing.

Percy spared no expense when it came to fox hunting. One particular truck even had a red police light mounted over the cab. The trucks also had dual exhaust pipes with "cherry-bomb" mufflers. I always went hunting with Percy when he asked me because it meant I would get to drive the trucks. He always started his truck with the gas pedal floored. When the engine started, it roared to life, and the loud cherry bomb mufflers let out a sigh of relief as the engine idled down from its boastful start. I liked riding with him because he drove very fast and sometimes even spun the tires.

Perry beside Percy Flowers's foxhound truck, mid-1960s

Perry standing on bumper of Percy's custom dog truck, holding his pocketknife, 1966

The Fox Hunt

I felt a tug at the blankets. It was Mama.

"Get up, son. He'll be here in a few minutes. He said he'd be here around four and you only got 'bout twenty minutes. I'm gonna fix you some biscuits to take with you while you getting ready."

I made my way up, got dressed, and went to the kitchen. Mama had the porch light on so he would know we were up. Our dog Spot began to bark and we heard Percy pull up into the driveway. The hunting hounds were loaded and they whimpered in the back of the truck. Occasionally one barked. Mama held the screen door open for me.

As I walked toward the door she pointed to the table and said, "Don't forget dem biscuits, Perry. They're there on the table in the sack. Y'all will enjoy them later."

As I stepped through the door to go outside, I instantly felt the cool morning nip in the air on my face and it drew me out of my sleepiness. It was completely dark outside except for the porch light and Percy's bright truck lights.

I opened the truck door and Percy said, "You hungry, Perry? We going to stop in Clayton and meet Joel for some breakfast."

I was sleepy and he could tell. "Perry, lay your head down, and I'll wake you up when I get to Clayton."

I leaned over and lay down on the bench seat. He placed his hand on my side and patted me, saying, "Don't worry. I'll wake you up when we get there."

Before long, Percy shook me and said, "We're here, Perry."

The seven-mile trip had gone by in an instant. I felt the truck tire bump the side curb as we parked on Main Street in Clayton by Western Auto, where we had recently purchased the little black mini-bike. Looking out the window, I saw the other dog truck—the double-decker one. Joel and the other men had already arrived and gone into the small hole-in-the-wall restaurant. We crossed the street and walked in to see two men sitting on the wooden benches at the table with Joel.

We took a seat at the next table. The waitress came over and asked, "Whatta you have?"

"Ah cup of coffee for me, and we will have some bacon and eggs and grits," Percy told her.

Joel and the other men already had their coffee. Percy told Joel, "We'll drive up to the same place we went last time in Chatham County."

Joel wasn't happy. "Well the coyotes are so damn bad out there."

Percy and Joel talked about where to "let out" the dogs once we got there. Before breakfast was over, the other men smoked a cigarette. One of them had a silver flip-open lighter. He sat it on the table while he smoked and flipped the top open and closed.

The waitress brought the bill to Percy, and he pulled out a wad of cash and paid her.

As we left, Joel said, "I'll have on the radio," referring to the CBs in the trucks. I climbed back into the truck and we pulled out of the parking spots and headed toward Chatham County. It was still pitch dark outside and I was still sleepy, so I lay down again to sleep. I woke up as Percy was maneuvering the truck onto a dirt path and over the path's washboard bumps. I looked up. The truck lights illuminated our way, but the fog was so thick that we couldn't see too far ahead of us.

Percy came up to a side road and pulled in there. "Perry, we'll let out right over there by that opening in the woods."

He swung the truck to the right, stuck his arm out the window, and motioned Joel ahead, pointing to an opening I could see from his headlights shining on it. Joel maneuvered his truck around us, running over a limb and snapping it with a loud pop. He pulled the double-decker ahead and shut off the lights and the engine. We pulled up and did the same. I didn't want to leave the warmth of the truck for the chilly, uncomfortable air.

The hounds were restless, and one barked. Joel hit the side of the truck and said, "Shut that fuss up!" The dogs quieted down except for the occasional whimper and the scuffle of their paws as they skittered inside the truck with excitement. Percy and Joel opened the double steel doors on the back of the truck bed cages and the dogs rushed out silently as if escaping from prison. Their paws pounded the ground as if a small army had just been unleashed. They headed directly for the woods, and in a minute all was quiet again.

"It won't be long before they jump one!" exclaimed Percy.

Joel agreed. "Yeaaaa, they gonna tear his ass up."

In just a few minutes, I was thinking about how cold I was when we heard a dog bray out with all his might. "Awllllllllllllll!! Awllllllllllllll!!"

"Hotta mighty no, told you it wouldn't be long," Percy exclaimed. In an instant, another shrill cry echoed out. "That's that bitch with the high-squealing mouth," he said, referring to the unique sound of each dog that he knew so well.

He knew all the dogs' "mouths" and could call them by name. He would say, "That's ole Corey," or, "That's a July bitch," or some other name. He knew what they would do before they did it. In another moment, several dogs grouped together as a pack, and the race for the fox began. The sound of the hounds was like a carefully orchestrated symphony. The high-pitch tone of the bitches was constant, steady, and rhythmic, punctuated by the deep chuffs of the dogs' deep throaty bays. They all sang in unison. There was no sound so beautiful to Percy than the high-pitched squeal from one of the dogs leading the pack.

Several minutes had passed when Percy said, "That's a gray fox they're after. We'll have a good race with him."

The dogs were giving the chase of their lives. Their voices brought light to the morning as the sun rose and gave view to a distant field just past the woods where we stood. Fog hovered over the field so thick that it was difficult to make out the ground. The dog's voices faded slightly as they chased the fox farther away.

Percy cupped his ears with his hands and listened for a moment. "Huh, yuh hear 'em?"

He headed for the truck. "Come on, Perry. Joel, dem dogs are going outta hearing. I'm going over behind that field."

He started the truck, as always allowing the loud engine to roar to life and then calm to idle. He threw the shifter into reverse just before the engine reached idle, and it jerked backward as he made a quick, backing turn-around. We rushed out onto the dirt road with tires spinning, and the truck slid slightly onto the road.

I thought to myself, *Now this is the real reason I like to come hunting—to go fast.*

He sped the truck down the dirt road as we reached a ninety-degree curve. The truck slid slightly, and we skidded across the washboard dirt road surface. We made a right turn and cut across some grass to drive next to a soybean field that ran along the woods. He switched the truck off as we were still rolling fast, the engine quieting as we coasted to a stop. Before we stopped, Percy opened the door and was out of the truck to listen. I could hear the dogs chasing after the fox, and Percy exclaimed excitedly, "Perry, they can go!"

Percy's body and soul seemed recharged from the morning hunt; he moved like a young boy. He reminded me of myself at Christmas. I'd never seen him move so fast. Again he cupped his ears. "Yes sar, they are tearing his ass up."

I agreed the chase was a beautiful sound, but as I listened I anxiously awaited the moment that he said I could drive the truck. We raced around the dirt roads over the next half hour and listened for the dogs. They went completely out of hearing, so we drove back to where Joel waited. Joel stood on top of the truck's dog cage, pointing in the direction where the dogs had run. Percy, as before, switched the truck off as we coasted to a stop and left the shifter in the neutral, exiting to listen.

*Percy Flowers (with foxhunting truck
shown in background)*

"Hotta mighty no, they are going to catch that fox, Joel. They're over there right back in that bean field. You better get over there before they catch him," he advised.

Both men started the trucks, and it was a hair-raising race back around the sharp curve and alongside the bean field to a stop. Everyone got out, and we heard the dogs in an all-time hard bellowing chase.

Percy was on top of the truck dog cage and said urgently to Joel, "He just crossed down there and hit that bean field. You better get out there. They gone catch that fox. If you want to get him, you better get out there now."

The hounds, a short time after Percy spotted the fox, tore out of the woods in a fiery, bellowing chase. I could see the beans sway as the hounds ripped through the field behind the fox. All went quiet as a single dog yelped.

"They got him, get out there!" Percy yelled to Joel. He turned to me. "Perry, you run out there and try to get to the dogs. Try to beat Joel's ass to them and get the fox. But be careful and not get bit."

I took off running through the soybean field. The beans were almost head high to me, making it difficult for me to pass through. I reached the spot where the dogs had quit running; several dogs passed by. All was quiet as I looked for the fox. I heard Joel say to one of the dogs, "Get back now."

I looked toward his voice, and there was Joel holding the fox high over his head, walking toward me on his way back to the truck. A dog followed as if waiting for a moment to swipe his trophy fox from the human thief. We walked back through the bean field to the truck, about three hundred feet away. When I walked out of the field, I was soaked with water from the morning dew on the beans. Joel and the dogs were wet, too. Joel showed the gray fox to Percy, and they discussed how well the dogs had performed.

Percy told me, "Now, Perry, that's one of the best races you'll ever hear in your life." As soon as he had gotten the words out of his mouth, we heard another deep bellow from a distance. "Awlllllllll! Awlllllllll!"

"They struck up another one," said Joel. By now the sun was well up in the eastern sky, and in the distance we spied the occasional car passing on the faraway paved road. The dogs that had just finished the chase and caught the fox heard the other dogs chasing the second fox and tore off to unite in that hunt. A similar race took place and again they caught a fox. It was turning out to be a successful day; two foxes had been caught by slightly past mid-morning! We'd spent an entire morning listening to the foxhounds race through woods and bean fields without any interruptions. As we tailed the second fox, Percy told Joel to start picking up the dogs.

"Perry, you want to drive?"

Those were the words I had waited for all morning! I was in the driver's seat to claim the steering wheel far before Percy could get in. I was delighted when he headed for the passenger side because then I knew I really was going to get to drive. I was just old enough to reach the pedals by myself. In the past, I'd sat in Percy's lap because I couldn't reach the accelerator and brake. I started the truck, just the way he always started it. The engine roared to life, and as the loud mufflers settled down I noticed him smiling at me. "Now back up and don't run over the man's beans, Perry."

I started backing up and glancing back through the dog cage to see my way clear.

"Perry, how do you turn your neck around so far? Boy, you can turn your neck like an owl. I shaw wish I could be as young and feel as good as you do."

Of course I stretched my neck even farther the next time I turned to look back. I pulled the truck out of the field and onto the dirt road, careful not to speed away as he had, fearing he may not think I was being careful enough. I didn't want to do anything to jeopardize my driving. As we neared the end of the long dirt road, he leaned over and put his brown-brim hat with the golden feather on my head. He said, "Now, Perry, if you see a law just keep driving and he won't even notice you. Turn right and there's a little store down here. We'll get us a Coca-Cola."

This was the grocery store where the clerk bragged to Percy's face that he used to buy whiskey from a moonshiner named Percy Flowers. "I knowed him good," he said, without, in fact, realizing he was speaking to the king himself.

After we got our Cokes and snacks, we went outside to sit on the over-extended tailgate bumper to eat and drink. It was close to noon and sunny as we shared the morning. He ate his potted meat and asked me to try some. I refused and he smiled, knowing that I would never try potted meat.

I often thought of how Percy chose his words and some of the things he said. For example, on the old white bench, while sitting on the store sidewalk, he said that he would give all he had to be my age just one more time. When I now sit alone and reflect upon our past, reliving these times, at this moment I too would give all that I own to have that day back just one more time, that moment, with just the two of us during a glorious day of fox hunting.

Josh and John, my words cannot convince you or describe to you how time seems so endless as a child and so short as an adult. The moments we spend together are precious. I hear Percy in my own voice as I often speak to you children. I now understand just how he felt and how you feel. Enjoy every moment and make each one last. Find that one thing in life that you love and be the very best that you can be at it. For Percy, "that one thing" was foxhound racing.

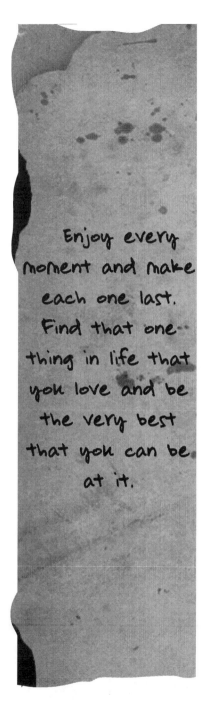

Enjoy every moment and make each one last. Find that one thing in life that you love and be the very best that you can be at it.

Percy Flowers and his foxhounds
stretch their legs

Percy Flowers, far left, and Curry Sullivan, far right, with prize-winning foxhound team

Percy Flowers with his team of breeders and trainers and a prize-winning hound at field trials

7

TOBACCO FARMING: HARD WORK CAME EARLY

Dear Josh and John,

Summers were filled with work and plenty of it. The fields needed disking, tobacco plants needed planting, corn and soybeans needed tending, and it all needed harvesting. Percy was used to hard work. As I've said before, he earned every single thing that he ever owned. For me, he expected the same. While many kids were at basketball practice, on summer vacation, or doing paltry chores in exchange for an allowance, I was driving tractors disking fields and working in tobacco fields. Men of that generation, especially Percy, believed that work was essential if you were ever going to amount to anything. Mama was just as influential as Percy when it came to work and wisdom. She was determined to steer me right and get me off of the farm using what limited knowledge of the world she had. Let me take you boys back to 1972 when I was your age...

Mama (Bea) said you needed "two thangs": an education and God. Mama only had a sixth-grade education, and Curry only finished the third grade. Percy had just a seventh-grade education. They all did fine. At least I thought so. I already was being "learned" stuff in school. My first-grade teacher and I had a debate. I had used a common word: "ain't."

"'Ain't' is not a word," she said.

"It is, too," I replied. "There is even three 'ain'ts.' 'Ain't' means a mama's sister, 'ain't' means a pee ain't, and 'ain't' is like 'I ain't going to do something.'"

She seemed to be hiding a smile.

I guess nobody ever learned her that word. Anyways, I knew teachers meant well, but, as I might have said back then, "Dey jis' didn't know everthang."

I demonstrated my superior intellect once again in the sixth grade when the teacher distributed a test booklet and asked the students to write their name in the top right corner on the booklet, and the phrase "IQ" at the top of the page. Dutifully, I wrote "Eye Que" and the teacher once again smiled and tapped her index finger on my booklet as she walked by. She must have thought I was exceptional.

Church was just more learning. We started going to Clayton Pentecostal Church. It was a little church in Clayton, about nine miles from our house. Preacher Beacham was the pastor. Ms. Cook was the Sunday school teacher, and Mama sang in the choir. We went to church every Sunday morning, Sunday night, and Wednesday night. I never liked going much, though. The singing was just OK. The choir always sang three songs before the preacher preached. I learned a lot of songs like "Down by the River" and "Jesus Is Coming Soon" and "The Old Rugged Cross."

Sometimes people sang solo and they weren't always on key. Some of them even needed some work staying in tune. The women all had their hair done up in big beehives. That was the trend then. It was also a sin for a woman to wear pants or use make-up. Seemed like a lot of things were sins but people did them anyways.

Mama always kept a pack of gum or a piece of candy in her purse that she would give us when the preacher was preaching. A lot of the old people "talked in tongues," and this scared me. One time my cousin Dinky went with us, and when they talked in tongues it scared him so much he ran out of church. Mama had to go get him. He never went again. His mama was dying from cancer and his father was a drunk, so Dinky stayed with us a lot.

On Wednesday nights church started at 7:30 p.m. and was supposed to be over by 9:00 p.m. There was a small clock that hung on the back wall, and I kept a sharp eye on it. Problem was, around five minutes till nine o'clock, Preacher Beacham would seem to bring the sermon to a close only to then say, "Like for you to join me at the altar to pray." I knew that meant that church could go for another hour because the old people would start talking in tongues. My prayer was simple but sincere. Around ten minutes to nine I'd start praying to Jesus that Preacher Beacham would please not call everybody to the altar. One time this worked, and I thought Jesus had heard my prayer. I left church feeling like my prayer had been answered and that I had a new relationship with God.

Church was a must for us children, and Sunday was chicken day. Every Sunday, Mama made fried chicken with mashed potatoes. She was known for her good cooking and sweet tea. I always wanted to be some place other than church. Nevertheless, it did lay the foundation for knowing right from wrong. It gave me a basic desire for and understanding of Christ that has guided me through the path of life ever since. The church teachings and Mama's words always stuck with me. She always said from the time I was young, "I sure hope to God that you get out of this place and make something of yourself someday. There's nothing here but a lot of hard work."

Tobacco work was just a lot of damn hard work. Mama worked in it and so she knew what she was talking about. My sister and I just stayed around the field or barn where Mama worked. Tobacco season started with pulling the plants to use on the "tobacco setter." There were small tobacco beds where the tobacco plants were grown to several inches tall in preparation for planting in the fields. The plants were pulled and used on the four-place setter from which they were planted in the fields, usually by women.

The tobacco setter was pulled behind a tractor at a snail's pace. Four seats on the planter faced backward and in front of each seat was a box where the plants were laid and straightened before being put on the planting wheel. On the side of the seat was a planting wheel with a small arm where each plant was placed. As the tractor pulled the planter, the wheel would turn and the riders would place plants onto the planting wheel. The wheel would roll and place the plants into the freshly prepared ground. I walked

119

behind the setter and filled in by hand spots that the setter missed putting a plant. It took the summer for the tobacco to grow over five feet tall. When it got tall, it had to be topped and suckered. Topping and suckering was done manually by walking down each row and breaking the flower out of the top of the tobacco plant. Usually eight or ten people walked through the fields and performed this tedious operation.

Often times Negros did a lot of the field work. I liked walking in the fields and finding fat green tobacco worms; they had a small horn like an antenna on the top of their heads. Most of the time I was barefoot and enjoyed the feel of the dirt under my feet. Sometimes I'd step on a dirt clod that would bend me over until I caught my balance again. My feet were pretty tough from going barefoot throughout the summers.

When the tobacco was ready to be taken out of the fields the bottom leaves would start to turn a deep shade of tan. These were known as the lugs. Men did the cropping, Negros and whites together. Cropping or priming meant pulling the leaves from the stalks. The croppers got a little more money per hour than the barn folks. They made $1.25 per hour. To haul the tobacco to the barns they used tractors and trailers. Young'uns, boys, drove the tractors. Women worked at the barns and looped the tobacco on a looping horse. A looping horse was a device that held a tobacco stick horizontal while the women used tobacco string to hand loop the individual handfuls of tobacco. By the 1970s, most farmers used large sewing machines to sew the tobacco on the sticks. The hangers were always men.

They would climb into the barn, one man over the other, and stand on tiers to the top of the barn. These tiers were made of wood and would flex as the men climbed on them. Although they were a permanent part of the barn, they were somewhat rickety. Sometimes the height of the barn could be thirty-five feet. There were no safety nets to catch the men if they slipped. These men would pass a stick of tobacco from one man up to the next until it reached the top of the barn where it was placed on the tiers. There the tobacco would hang and be cured by burners in the barns fed by diesel fuel. Early on, my sister and I just stayed close to Mama for the first few summers because we were too young to really work.

One summer while at the barn on Highway 42, Mama and a Negro woman were looping tobacco. It was a hot summer day, and a wasp stung my sister on the arm. The old Negro lady who was dipping snuff spat on the sting and said the juice would stop the sting. Guess she was right, but the tobacco spit looked nasty on the sting—and hanging from her lip after she spat. Back then a lot of people chewed tobacco and dipped snuff.

By ten years old I was a tractor driver in the fields and I pulled the trailer of tobacco up and down the roads from the fields to the barns. I knew how to stay with the croppers just right. At first a cropper may yell to hold up. If I got too far in front of the croppers, they had to carry the tobacco too far and waste time. There were no bosses in the field. You either "stayed up" (kept up) or didn't work.

Bud, who seemed old to me at the time, was one of the fastest croppers. He stayed in front of the other croppers and would help the others finish out their rows sometimes. Bud was a white man, never married, and known to be just a little off. He often answered the affirmative as, "Yep, yep, yep, yep," very fast. Everyone liked Bud. A lot of the croppers came back every year and were mostly Negros from the local area of Red Hill. They worked hard. They sang a lot, and I sang with them. Slave days may have ended, but the lifestyle carried on in the tobacco fields of North Carolina.

When I wasn't working tobacco, I disked the fields on a red Massey Ferguson 1100. Farmers pull rows of large metal disks behind their tractors to deeply cut the top layers of the hard earth in order to loosen the soil. I drove a ninety-plus-horsepower tractor, big for the time. The disk was from a Caterpillar, yellow and heavy duty. I even did some plowing with a Ferguson 135. I didn't do much plowing because Percy had caught me experimenting with the tractor. I would lower the plow into the soft earth with the hand controls, causing the plow to dig deep into the ground. This forced the front wheels off the ground. It was fun; I learned how to wheelie a tractor. I could wheelie a tractor until the motor bogged down. Problem was, Percy saw it and that was the end of that.

Disking with the Massey 1100 was my favorite. I couldn't reach the clutch while on the seat, so I'd slide off the seat to stand on the clutch or brake. The clutch was hard to push on the 1100, so I had to lean against the seat and press with all my might. Since I couldn't hold it long, I'd quickly throw the shifter to neutral or first gear and let up on the clutch. John D., the Tractor Man, was brave. He would let me back the large 1100 up to the disk as he hooked it up. It took quite a bit of precision to mate the tractor receiver with the large disk. At times my leg was so tired that it would shake as I held the clutch with all my might. To let go of the clutch would catapult the tractor over John D. and the disk. He never knew how close he came to me backing over him. He was lucky.

I even knew how to fill the tractor with diesel and check the oil, pump up the tires, and clean the air breather. When in the field disking, I'd hop down to press the large clutch, put it in first gear, and push full forward on the throttle. The large diesel engine would roar and bellow black smoke. As I slowly let the clutch out, the tractor tires would slightly spin as the large cat disk sunk into the dirt. The front end would bounce a little until it settled down and was going good. I knew how to disk as well as any man.

One day I was disking the field beside the old home place on Buffalo Road when a piece of the muffler blew off and went down my shirt. The big tractor was on its own as I scrambled to get the hot metal out of my shirt. It left a scar that I still have today. That same day Percy and Reno drove up to the field to surprise me with a root beer milkshake and hotdog from the Tastee-Freez in Clayton. Percy knew I liked root beer milkshakes and would drive all the way to Clayton to get me one when I was disking. I disked a lot of land, and Percy even paid me.

When I was big enough to crop, I cropped. In the mornings we started a little after sunrise. The large leafy tobacco plants were wet with morning dew, and the cold mornings could be hard on me as a child. I would shiver and shake, wishing for the warm bed I had just left. Still, it didn't take long to wish it were still wet as the sun rose and the summer temperatures climbed. The tobacco became sticky and released all its tar and gum as you cropped it. The gum was brown like tobacco spit, and it got into your hair, clothes, and skin. Nothing would take the brown out of your hands, not even gasoline or kerosene. It had to wear off. Good thing I didn't crop during school. The other kids would have teased me. By the age of twelve or thirteen years old, I could keep up with most of the men.

The days were long. The best time was break, around nine thirty or ten o'clock. There was not a set time. It was when the barn man sent the dranks and nabs (Lance-type crackers) out on a trailer. Breaks were fun. Pepsi, Mountain Dew, or RC was normal with an orange nab or moon pie. The old men poked fun at each other and told jokes, usually about somebody not able to stay up or something about women. Sometimes they talked about the women at the barn. Richard Petty and Cale Yarborough or Ford versus Chevy could either start an argument or lead to a bet.

Some men sang during the day or whistled. Sometimes all of them sang. I really liked that because it made it easier to be in the field. It wasn't like now with work rules and breaks all the time. You worked hard and took a break one time in the morning and one time in the afternoon with an hour lunch. If you could crop fast enough to send a trailer to the barn before another one arrived, then you could stop for a few minutes. That was it. Quitting time was when the work was finished. And that was when Mr. Wallace, the farmer, said it was.

Mama worked at the barn on the sewing machine. The looping horse had been replaced with this huge sewing machine for sewing the tobacco onto the stick. Usually four women would take the tobacco from the trailer that was parked about two feet from the sewing machine and place it on the sewing machine conveyor belt. The women stood between the sewing machine and the trailer and had to turn around every time to get the tobacco. Two women would place a bundle of tobacco on the conveyer belt, someone would place a tobacco stick on that layer, and the other two women would place a bundle of tobacco over the top of the stick. I never considered before just how many times Mama turned around in a day. The tobacco would travel down the sewing machine and go through a large sewing needle that sewed the bundles to the stick. Sometimes the string would break, stopping the work until someone rethreaded the needle. After the tobacco was sewn onto the sticks it was passed to the hangers for hanging in the barns. When the barn was full, the fuel-oil burners were lit and the tobacco was cured, a process that could take more than a week. Once it was cured, the tobacco was removed from the barn one stick at a time, threads cut and sticks removed.

Then came the sheeting. Someone would place a large tobacco basket about four feet across on the ground and then lay a large burlap tobacco sheet inside of it. Women took off the cured tobacco leaves from the sticks and placed them onto the large burlap sheets. When they had filled the basket they pulled the four corners of the sheet together and then tugged some more to tie the corners into knots.

With the tobacco sheeted, it was ready to go to the warehouse for sale. It was common to see a large, two-ton flatbed truck loaded with burlap bundles of tobacco, the load swaying as it went down the road.

Mama's hands often had blisters from all the work. Percy owned all of the land and tenant farmers paid to lease his land. Mr. Wallace was just one of several who farmed the thousands of acres. I knew that this was hard work and, as I've said before, I will always remember how Mama said, "I want you and your sister to get a education and get out of this place someday."

Josh and John, those days of hard work seemed endless at the time. We didn't have PlayStations, iPods, or Xboxes for entertainment. In fact, we had just received our first telephone with a party line. Now that was entertainment.

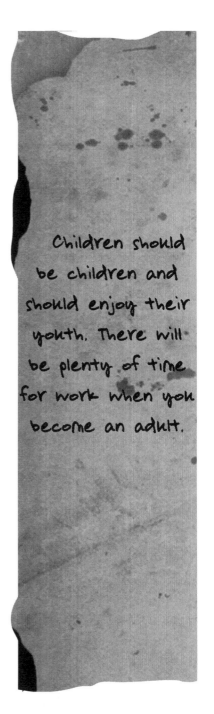

Children should be children and should enjoy their youth. There will be plenty of time for work when you become an adult.

126

The point is, I worked very, very hard at outdoor labor—as a child. I believe it is important for you two to develop a solid work ethic. There is a value to hard work. But, it is my hope that you will never have to work at hard physical labor as we did, especially while you are still children. Children should be children and should enjoy their youth. When you become an adult, there will be plenty of time for work.

That was just how it was on a tobacco farm in the South.

8

WINE AND THE THREE MURDERERS

Dear Josh and John,

I tell you this story so that you may know that people can be cruel and void of pity and emotion. You have always been shielded by a good home and softer and gentler people than the ones I grew up with and heard stories about. You should know that times were not always so easy and kind. Justice was harsh, and it wasn't always the courts doing the judging and dealing out the sentences. Never underestimate anyone.

One winter's day I asked Ole Wine why he always limped. Wine wasn't so fast to talk as I pressed for an answer.

I Tole You Dat I Was Gone Kill You: Wine's Tale

Ole Wine was a large Negro man who walked with a limp. Every winter he came to our house and helped kill and clean hogs. Wine was direct and used simple words. He seemed easygoing and gentle in nature. What he said he meant. Back then, men seemed more fierce and unbridled than now. Let me take you back there to the time of Wine and the three murderers. These are two stories lost and forgotten that were probably never recorded.

One day Wine was limping around and struggling to pierce the hind leg of a hog's carcass with the tripod hook. Once the hooks were in, the men would use the tripod to hoist the hog into the air. As he limped around, as he always did, I asked Wine about his leg and why he limped. Wine eased his old marred face toward Curry and lifted his eyes to focus on him as he talked. Wine's skin was a deep dark black and his lips were abnormally thick, jutting downward so that his bottom lip hung open exposing the red and purple inside. His eyelids hung down making the edge of the lids look red like an old hound dog looking up after a long nap.

Wine began to explain why his leg hurt.

"Uh ole dam nigger shot me one night when I wuz walkin' by his house. He said he thought I wuz another nigger. He said he was drunk and didn't know it was me. But I tole dat dam nigger dat one day I wuz gone kill him for shooten me in my knee. My leg hurts ever' day since he shot me."

Curry just nodded, and they continued to work at hooking the hog carcass to the tripod. The man who'd shot Wine lived just down the road from him.

Seven years had passed since Wine had been shot, and he'd worked, limped, and sweated through various farm jobs. Wine and his "shooter" had talked many times since the incident. One day over the weekend after a long week of work, Wine was sitting at his dining room table and peering out the window into the woods when his wife came in.

"Hey, you gone cook fo' dem dis evening?" Wine was referring to the shooter and his wife. Wine had asked them to come for supper. Seven years had passed and they had apparently gone from antagonists to friends.

"Yea, we gone have sum'in and they gone be here after ah while." She was planning on making fried chicken, collards, and biscuits.

Wine returned his stare toward the window and said no more. A while passed as his wife prepared the modest meal for their guests. The whole time Wine went about his business as normal. Then, the guests arrived, having walked from their house to Wine's. It was only a quarter mile or so. As they stepped up onto the wooden porch, the boards creaked slightly.

"Hey, we here, Wine. Ya home?" called the shooter. Wine limped to the screen door and opened it for the shooter and his wife to enter.

"Something sho' smells good here," said the shooter. The two women were happy to see one another and talked in the kitchen. Wine and his shooter walked to the front porch and sat beside each other. The shooter did most of the talking as Wine just gave an occasional "un huah."

A few minutes passed and Wine's wife called the two men. "It ready. Y'all come on in."

The two men slowly lifted themselves from the small chairs. Wine opened the screen door, the steel spring squeaking from the pull. The table was set for four with a plate of homemade biscuits in the center and a glass of water for each person. Wine got up and left the table while his wife continued to bring out the food. The shooter was sitting where Wine had sat earlier when he stared out into the woods.

Wine returned to the kitchen and without warning raised his buckshot-loaded shotgun and unloaded the shotgun, point blank, into the back of his friend's head. The sound of the shotgun was deafening, and it all occurred in an instant. The shooter's brains and face were splattered all over the dinner table, wall, and windows. The women were petrified as they stared at Wine standing over the slumped body of his former friend.

Wine simply said, "I tole you dat I wuz gone kill you, nigger."

He took the shotgun and placed it in the corner of the room behind a door and walked to the porch where he sat down in his chair. The passing years had done nothing to dampen the fire of revenge. He spent some years in the state penitentiary, and after his release he returned to our area and kept working for Percy and killing hogs for us each winter. He had already served his time when I knew him and asked about his leg.

Curry was working at the store one day when Percy came in and said, "Wine's gone."

"Where'd he go?" Curry asked.

"He's gone on. He's dead. I went up to his house to pick

him up to work and when I got there his grandson met me at the door. I walked in and Ole Wine was sitting in the chair leaned back. His boy said he thought he was dead. I just said, 'Yep, he's dead alright.' The little children was still sitting by his chair and his wife was outside working."

Wine had died of natural causes sitting in his chair as his grandchildren played by his feet.

Miss Lynch and the Three Murderers

Besides Wine, there was another killing years earlier as told to me by Curry. It went something like this. Three Negros were working a sawmill down in the woods by the store. It was brutally hot and sweat beaded on the men's dark skin, dripping from their brows as they maneuvered the logs toward the cutting blade. The loud buzz of the large saw blades spinning and cutting through the hard logs enveloped the whole space. The men were strong and chiseled from the laborious work.

Just up the hillside was a small white-boarded house where Miss Lynch lived. In the backyard was a large stack of chopped wood for heating. Her husband was a drunk and abusive. Miss Lynch, however, was known as a gentle woman, one of the kindest souls around. She felt some sorrow and pity for the hard-working men and sometimes offered them water. Miss Lynch's husband was away one day when she sat an apple pie on the back porch to cool. It was close to lunchtime and she knew the Negros would come by soon and sit and eat some lunch close by the woodpile in her backyard. She had planned to give the pie to them along with some water.

Along the small footpath came the three Negros to take a quick lunch break. As they passed, Miss Lynch motioned to them to come up for the water. They approached her as usual, and she gave them water. As she reached down from the porch to hand them the pie, one of the Negros grabbed her wrist and jerked her from the porch. The three men took her into the edge of the woods and all three raped her.

When they had finished with her, one of the Negros picked up the axe and split her head like a piece of wood.

Two of the men fled the area attempting to escape their doom. Miss Lynch's husband arrived and found her body sprawled by the woodpile. He summoned some of the local men and told them what had happened. The group of men gathered at the house and began a search of the area. They found one of the men hiding in the back of a small shed by the sawmill. They forced him out, guns drawn. In an effort to save his own life, he told them that the other two men had headed for the train station by Smithfield.

Miss Lynch's husband said, "I just want the first shot." He took the rifle and aimed at the Negro and pulled the trigger. He told the others to finish it. Ole Man Josh had two bloodhounds, and he took the two hounds to the scene to track the two Negros. The other men headed for the train station. As they arrived at the train station, the train was pulling away. They rushed in to find that two Negros were on board. The men jumped into their trucks and raced to the track crossing down the road. They managed to stop the train by flagging it down. They entered the train armed with anger and shotguns. One of the Negros managed to escape from the train before it stopped. The other was not so fortunate. The men took the Negro to a nearby tree and shot him to death. Authorities apprehended the remaining Negro and jailed him. He was later tried and sent to the state penitentiary. A man in the community collected money from locals and apparently hired a prisoner in the state penitentiary to kill the remaining Negro. He lived less than three weeks once he arrived in prison.

In those days, men were hard and cold and filled with resolve. Their words were harsh and they meant them. Work was the norm and loafers were mostly outcasts. Ole Wine worked hard to make a living. His shooter took from him one of the few things he had: his health. To Ole Wine, his revenge was justified, and the shooter paid for his crime. With the three murderers, community justice was swift and accepted. Curry told me the story as a matter of fact with nary a hint of emotion or concern.

Josh and John, never prejudge anyone, but never underestimate anyone either. So many times, if you listen, you will hear something you never expected. Plus, you cannot know a person's heart. You can only know what he or she allows you to know. The person's intentions, good or bad, are not always clear. And life is like seasons, always changing. What you do

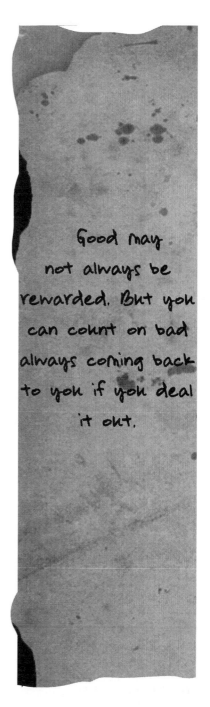

Good may not always be rewarded. But you can count on bad always coming back to you if you deal it out.

137

today will seem strange years down the road. You should try to always stay steady and grounded in good and fair ways. You should never be reckless when dealing with people and always be considerate. Good may not always be rewarded. But you can count on bad always coming back to you if you deal it out.

9

CHANGING COURSE

Dear Josh and John,

  By ten years old, I was the youngest man alive. My Aunt Leatrice told Mama that I acted just like the men at the store. That's where I spent all my time, so why shouldn't I act like a man? Spitting, whistling, cussing, hunting, I knew it all. Mama said, "Son, I sure hope you leave this farm and don't grow up like these people 'round here. You need to make something of yourself. Lord, I hope you and Tammy can get away from this place before it's too late." Mama was a religious woman, and she often referred to the Lord in all she did.

I knew all about farming, driving tractors, foxhound racing, cockfighting, and people. Listening to Percy and all the old men around the store, I had learned how to size a person up in just a few minutes. At least I thought so. It was common for me to say or do just like the men at the store. Keep in mind these were men of the old generation and saw the folks of the 1970s as worthless, weak, and void of morality and work. They made their thoughts known and were loose-tongued around me even though I was a kid. I knew that long hair was for girls, boys carried pocketknives, and hippies were all dope addicts.

I was ready to be a real man. I was ready to set out on a different course.

In 1972, the hippie generation was still going strong and motorcycles were symbolic of their generation. Dirt track motocross racing was very popular among the youth. Mama was against motorcycles because her brother had been killed on one. Curry had no opinion either way. At least he dared not say. Furthermore, Percy was against motorcycles because he felt that they were too dangerous and were representative of a group of moral degenerates.

Every time Percy and I saw long-haired men he would say, "Look-uh there at that long-haired son of a bitch with nothing better to do than ride up and down the roads and smoke that dope." Well, he left no doubt about how he felt about long hair and motorcycles. Never mind that his grandsons were operating a motocross track just across the Neuse River within riding distance of my house.

I was starting to question the old-time social order and became interested in motorcycles even though I knew how Percy felt about them. Curry rarely spoke about anything, so he didn't present a problem for me racing. Percy had already purchased me a mini-bike a couple of years before, so how could he say no to another one now? I pleaded for a new motorbike, and reluctantly he agreed. He said, "Perry, you just won't listen. That damn thing is going to hurt you. You are more hardheaded than I ever was."

Well I didn't really believe that. Besides, he could be hardheaded, too. He was only concerned as any parent should be. We drove the big Cadillac to Honda of Raleigh some fifteen miles northwest of Clayton. We walked into the cycle shop to see a store full of new Japanese Hondas. Sitting on the floor was a shiny new yellow Honda Minitrail

50. It had fold-down handlebars and could fit into the big Cadillac trunk with no problem.

Percy purchased the motorbike and insisted that I get a helmet. "You better get a helmet or you might bust yur head open on dat thang," he cautioned. I chose a half-shell blue one.

A man placed the little Minitrail in the trunk of the Cadillac, and we went back home. It cost around $180. We arrived home, and he pulled to the backyard behind our house. He parked next to a large oak tree under the shade to shield us from the hot summer sun. I'll always remember that day.

He chewed on his White Owl cigar and said only, "Now, Perry, don't let this thang hurt you. It can."

He opened the large door, and I slid out behind him on the driver's side, so eager to see the new minibike. He opened the trunk, reached in, struggled a little, and finally unloaded the little yellow Minitrail 50. It was gleaming clean with chrome fold-down handlebars and an on/off switch on the gas cap. He showed me how to turn on the gas and kick-start it. He now seemed as excited as I was. His joy must have come from seeing me so happy. I remember his smile with the cigar between his teeth and his brim hat pushed up slightly from his struggle unloading the bike. He was wearing a button-up white shirt with cigar burns on the chest. He just watched and smiled as I rode around the yard on it. He told me not to tell anybody that he'd bought it, that his wife "would tear [his] ass up if she knowed."

I worshiped the Minitrail 50 and rode it every chance until it was worn out. In September 1972, I rode the small minibike to the motocross track near my home, taking an extra gas can with me to have enough gas to ride all day and enter a race. As I approached the track entrance I could hear all types of motorcycles roaring off into the woods around the track. I explained to the gate man that Percy said I didn't have to pay. They allowed me to pass. I went to the announcer's stand, gave my name, and entered the race for minibikes. It was a glorious sunny clear day—perfect racing weather.

As I revved up on the starting line, I was full of the confidence and vigor of a young warrior. I knew my skills were better than anyone else's. I had the stubbornness and stamina to see this through. But the reality of the race was a bit different from what I'd expected. As the flag came down, the dirt clods kicked up by the large knobby tires from the Bultacos, Huskys, CZs, and Maicos flew into my face and nearly knocked me off my bike. I choked on the fumes.

Funny thing was, this didn't discourage me but instead made me mad. "Dem sons a bitches!" I let out as the bikes passed me. I finished third and won a cup trophy. I still have it. I took the little minibike, the gas can, and trophy and rode home.

On the way home, crossing the Highway 42 Neuse River Bridge, a highway patrolman stopped me for riding the minibike on the highway. I explained it was the only way I had to get to the races. After promising not to do it again, he allowed me to go free. I was so excited to show the trophy to Mama. She told Percy, and he came over to see it.

He said to Mama, "That boy can go!" and "I hear ya, Perry."

Those were all encouraging words from him. Curry never even acknowledged me going to the races. He did look over at the trophy but just walked past it without a word. Within a year, Percy and I made another trip to Honda of Raleigh and purchased another motorcycle, an SL-70. I quickly stripped off the lights, cut off the muffler, and headed to the racetrack. My racing years had begun and an escape from the farm life was taking shape. Motorcycles were now in my blood as much as hunting and cockfighting were part of Percy's. Racing became a venting outlet of sorts, and riding was as natural as breathing for me. Mama didn't approve completely, but she let me do it, and Curry kept quiet. Work on the farm continued, but I was quickly changing course.

The next few years were filled with competition racing every weekend. Percy supported me with yet another motorbike, a Honda XR-75. By 1973, my talent had come into its own. Just down the road in Smithfield, a new Indian motorcycle shop opened. I begged Mama to take me to see it and try to get a sponsorship. She reluctantly did. Jim Steckenrider greeted us. Jim had just gotten out of the Navy as an operator aboard nuclear submarines. He was quiet, clean-cut, and very considerate. His attitude was markedly different from the hell-raisers I was accustomed to.

I looked over the small shop and must have seemed the brashest, most self-important, most confident boy alive.

I bragged to Jim about my supreme riding ability and negotiated a sponsorship as though I actually had some authority. Jim must have been secretly amused. He could surely see by our clothes that we needed the help. He actually offered me a full sponsorship to give me a try. Jim made a special modified Indian minibike that was just for racing. He stripped down a little Indian street bike, put on some knobby tires, and it was ready.

The first race was a disaster. I arrogantly blamed the bike, assigning the loss to an underpowered engine. Jim was always calm and had a way of talking to me so that I would come around to his way of thinking. He never raised his voice or criticized. This was a fairly new approach from what I had seen. Unfortunately, I took it as a weakness and continued my ranting most of the time. Over the next three years, Jim and I became closer and closer. He built bikes that were superior to the others at the track. He was more than just a calm voice of reason. Jim had a talent for invention and dedicated those talents toward building fast, reliable race bikes. He was a designer and knew how to tweak things to get the very most out of them. While he modified bikes and built his business, he continued to show incredible patience with me. We went on to win many races. In one summer, we won twenty-nine straight races. Jim was a friend and the second role model in my life. Even though I was too high-strung and proud to appreciate his intellect, he patiently encouraged me to be better.

By 1975, Jim moved to Illinois. Before he left, he organized a new sponsorship that would carry me on to win the United States National Championship at High Point Lucas

Raceway in Pennsylvania. For several years, competition racing occupied my every thought. Racing eventually consumed many of my weekends, and, due to sponsorship and traveling, slowly drew me away from the regular visits to the store. My absence did not sit well with Percy. Mama often told me that Percy wanted to know when I was coming home.

By 1979 my racing career was winding down. I had raced several years with much of the time between 1974 and 1978 spent away from home. Those few years of racing felt like a lifetime, and my interest began to wane. Furthermore, Percy was aging and in poor health. I returned to the farm just in time to revisit the old ways I had been so accustomed to.

As I fell back into the ways of farm life, it all looked different somehow. The few years racing and traveling had shed light on other ways to live. I had met and worked with professional

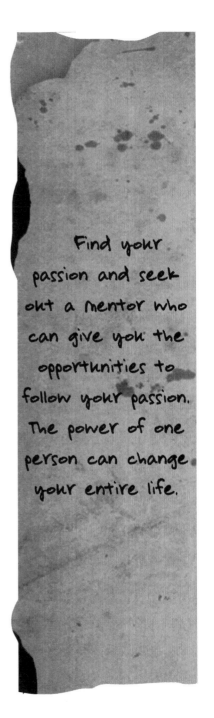

Find your passion and seek out a mentor who can give you the opportunities to follow your passion. The power of one person can change your entire life.

sponsors and businessmen who had guided me to national events and rare success for a young boy. They had not only let me do the sport I loved, they also introduced me to banking, management, and financing, and they had stressed the importance of a college education. Mama's dream was being answered. The door had been opened to a world outside of the farm. I passed through that door, never to return except for a brief visit.

Josh and John, motorcycle racing felt right for me. There was never any doubt in my mind that this was the one thing I loved and enjoyed as a child, and that I was the best at. When an opportunity arises in your life, you must recognize it and find a mentor who can give you the opportunities to follow your passion. The power of one person can change your entire life. The opportunity may not arrive in the package you expected it to, but you will know in your heart if it is for you. When you find your passion, run with it and never look back.

Perry Sullivan winning the United States National Motocross event

*Perry Sullivan qualifying for a na-
tional event as his cycle breaks in
half over a jump*

10

MAKING WHISKEY: THE LITTLE GIANT

Dear Josh and John,

The racing was slowing down, and my interests slowly returned to the farm for a brief time. For nearly four years, I had raced motocross and quietly slipped out of the farm life while traveling and competing in the eastern states. Sponsorships had revealed a glimpse of the legal side of businesses and the "normal life" of middle-class America. By comparison, the farm seemed like the Wild West—a place where everyone just shot from the hip.

Percy's moonshining lifestyle offered privileges and benefits that were attractive and fascinating to a young man. His life was raw and unbridled, quite a contrast from the law, order, and regulation that characterized the world of motorcycle racing. When I returned, Percy seemed old, with nearly all of his years behind him. I felt guilty about having been gone so often and realized that the cost would be years missed from Percy and the store life that could never be replaced. Being back, I wanted to be just like Percy. Being like him meant learning to make money by making moonshine.

Building the Little Giant

As a teenager, I had visited Percy's whiskey stills with Reno and had seen firsthand his large-scale, steam-still operation. I remember the immense boiler, over eight feet tall, with a large several-hundred-gallon pre-heater that rested on top. The cooker that sat beside the boiler held several hundred gallons of mash. The mash and cooling condensers were all fed by gas-powered engine pumps. When the still was running, whiskey flowed like water running from a garden hose. Percy's moonshining steam outfit could produce hundreds of gallons of whiskey per day.

Although I had seen Percy's mass whiskey-making operation, he had forbidden me from learning how to make moonshine. I had badgered Percy many times to teach me how to make whiskey, always knowing there would be the same answer.

"Perry, you need to forget about that whiskey and get a good education. You fuck around in whiskey, you will end up in jail. Thangs ain't like they use to be when I was in it. Dar was money in it then, and you could count on people. Money could keep your ass out of the pen. Hell fire, with a little money, anybody would be your friend. Back then nobody had nothing and a dollar meant something. The government has so many people workin' fur dem dat you can't trust nobody. Billy's best friend for seven years sent his ass up. He was an informant and sent all them boys to the pen. You forget about this whiskey making and let me send you to veterinarian school in Raleigh. I can git you in up there. You'll make a fortune and not have to have the problems I've had with the law. I don't want you to ever mess with whiskey. Don't drank it or fuck with it in any way or you just asking for trouble."

Percy's advice was solid and good. But a curious and persistent teenager wanted to walk in his shoes, a naive teenager who had already won a National Motocross Championship and who believed there was nothing he could not do. Surely if Percy had made a successful career of making whiskey then I could. After all, I was like him. After some more pleading, I convinced him to at least teach me how to make whiskey. Years before, he would never have allowed someone to wear him down like I did. Perhaps he felt there was a lesson here.

"Perry is going to worry me to death if we don't show him how to make whiskey. Howard [Reno], go get that little cooker out of that bottomland behind my house and take it to the welding shop in Smithfield. Have the ole man make a boiler, doubling keg, purifier, and worm. Then show him how to make it. Dat ah make a good little steam outfit. Work him and show him what it's all about and maybe he will leave it alone."

Reno glanced over with a little smile and said, "Yes sar!"

He went and got the small stainless steel cooker that had lain in the wet bottomland for years, unknown even to me. It was as though a long-lost treasure had been resurrected from the ground. Even though the cooker was old, it looked new and undamaged. It was a forty-gallon cooker, about three feet in diameter with the sides about two feet tall. At the bottom was a hole for a pipe outlet with a blow-out valve assembly. At the top was a smaller-diameter cylinder-shaped stack that made up the top of the cooker. The top stack was about ten inches in diameter and twelve inches high. On the top of the stack sat a bolt-on concave top with a 1½-inch hole in the very top. The top was bolted on with a rubber gasket between the cap and the rest of the cooker. It was beautiful. It looked like a hat made just for the cooker. We loaded the cooker in the back of a pickup truck and hauled it to Smithfield for the rest of the steel parts to be manufactured and matched to it. The cooker was the heart and soul of the still, where the whiskey would be distilled from the mash.

When we arrived at the welding shop, it was a surprise to find it located on the edge of Highway 70 at the entry of town. It was an old concrete-block building with a dirt parking lot. For some reason, I'd imagined it would be hidden on some backwoods farm. Reno went inside with me beside him. A man approached us and talked with Reno. The man's face and neck had evidently suffered some horrific damage as evidenced by disfigurement and scars. I couldn't help but stare as he talked. He occasionally glanced at me as if a youngster shouldn't be there. Reno explained what needed to be done, and the man agreed, seeming to know exactly what to do as if he had done this before. He said to give him about five days and he would have it ready. We left the cooker there and returned to the store.

*The little giant moonshine
steam still*

Back at the store, Reno said he had to talk to Percy and decide where to "set up the little giant." "Giant" was a name for whiskey stills. As we entered the store, Percy was sitting in a chair, resting. Reno walked over to him, gave a little wink with a slight head nod, and made a small hand motion as if to say, "Follow me." We all walked between the walk-in freezer and ice cream box, proceeding to the kitchen and office area. This area was secluded from the store traffic, a private area in the back of the store where Reno and I cooked and ate gnat meat and made chocolate or pineapple cakes. It seemed that secrecy was the order of the day.

Percy quickly asked, "What'd he say?"

Reno replied by holding up five fingers and saying, "Days." Reno said that we should go ahead and set up the barrels of mash because it would take about seven days to work off and by then the little giant would be ready. Percy and Reno talked in a low voice, unlike I'd ever heard them use before. This was all serious business. Reno listened intently and rubbed his head as they discussed a location to set up the little giant. They discussed the Pearsall Farm and a location toward Wilson's Mills. At the Wilson's Mills location was a natural spring in the woods back of the main road behind the dog pen.

Percy ultimately picked the natural spring. He said that would be the best place since the law had been on the Pearsall Farm. Percy told Reno, "Make sure we got some corn meal and sugar to set up four barrels. That ought to give a good four cases with that little giant. It'uh run four barrels easy. Thatta be about right. What you think?"

"Yes sar, dat's about right." Reno rubbed his hand back and forth over the top of his head and up and down his face as he considered what we needed. "Hmmm, let me see, fo' barrels, two hundred pounds ah sugar and ah hundred pounds of kone meal. I go down to da mill and get some meal ground up and we gots the sugar."

Percy smiled and said, "That ah be a good little operation for him to learn on."

"Some barrels in the barn and we ah burn um out and git um ready," Reno reminded him.

"OK, we better git on down to Atkinson's Mill and get the corn meal," Percy said. Atkinson's Mill was an old mill located on the river just a few miles from the store. Reno nodded up and down with a determined look over his face and just replied, "Um huh."

As we left the kitchen, Reno said, "Come on, Dino. Me and my boy gots ah little work to do." As we passed the store counter, Reno got some stick matches from the cigarette counter. I followed and we went out to the old barn next to the store. In the back of the barn in a stall sat fifty- and hundred-gallon whiskey barrels. I had seen them before and knew that they were there because I had played there. There were about fifty barrels in the stall. We looked them over and picked out four.

"Smell that, Dino, my boy," Reno said.

I leaned over one of the barrels and smelled the strong presence of whiskey. "Yea, that smells good, don't it?" I said.

Reno smiled as we began separating the four fifty-gallon barrels from the rest. We pulled them out and laid them on their sides behind the barn. Reno directed me to get some straw from the barn. I collected the straw and put some in each barrel.

"We gots ta burn um out or the mash won't work off," Reno explained. He leaned over and set fire to the straw in the first barrel and gave me the matches to light the others. The straw began to burn and, surprisingly to me, the inside of the barrels began to burn quickly. We rolled the barrels slightly to keep from burning just one area. The smell of the whiskey came out of the barrels as if we were performing some exorcism over them. In just a few minutes, the flames had burned the insides to char-black.

"They's ready now!" Reno exclaimed. We let the fires burn out and then set the barrels aside. Reno went to get the old Ford truck and backed it under the barn and loaded several bags of field corn that had been harvested over the summer.

"C'mon, Dino. Let's us go to da mill." We rode just a few miles to Atkinson's Mill, where we went inside to meet a man about grinding the corn. The man unloaded the bags of corn and took it to be ground. In just a short time, we had fresh-ground cornmeal. I looked into the bag; the corn had been ground to a fine mash and it smelled really good. The man loaded the corn onto the truck and we returned to the store where we stashed the cornmeal in the back of the store.

A few days later, Reno told me the giant was ready. We returned to the welding shop but this time in an old green Ford two-ton, aluminum-box truck. The old Ford always sat at the end of the parking lot, pulled over off of the lot, in an area grown over with grass and weeds. The truck bed was a large aluminum box nearly twenty feet long and tall enough for a man to stand up and have plenty of headroom. The back of the bed was secured with two large aluminum doors locking from the middle with a lever. I stepped up on the running board to open the passenger door. It squeaked as it opened, as if it hadn't been used for a long time. Reno climbed into the driver's side. There was a long stick shift that extended from the floor up about two feet, comfortable to the driver's reach. Located on the side of the shifter, by the shifting knob, was a red button about one inch in diameter. The red button was used to help shift the split axle. A push or pull on the red button would shift axle gears. The seat was dusty along with the green metal dashboard. You could write your name in the dust almost any place in the cab. There were smudge marks over the windshield where someone had wiped dew off at some point. The floorboard was all rubber with a piece torn away exposing the metal underneath. Dirt and dust covered it all.

Reno patted the accelerator several times and said, "C'mon now, let's go, ole girl," as if he were talking good luck into the truck.

The big Ford motor turned over slowly several times and then came to life. It was loud and sounded robust. Pushing the strong clutch down raised Reno a little off the seat. He worked the long shifter forward, backward, and side to side before finding first gear. As he slowly let out on the strong clutch, the old Ford bucked a little and slowly pulled out of its resting place and onto the parking lot. The brakes always made a *shhhhh* sound when pressed. We pulled out onto Highway 42 and made a turn towards Smithfield. The truck motor revved, but we were not moving very fast. Reno shifted the gears using the shifter, followed by a pull or push on the red knob. I could hear the transmission and the axle switch gears as the old Ford bucked with each shift.

Reno showed me all the gears as we accelerated. He obviously liked shifting the gears as he said, "Now dis is a real truck, Dino."

We met the same man again at the welding shop. He was the owner, and this had been a job for the owner's eyes only and not for his workers. We followed him into the shop and found the boiler, doublin' keg, purifier, and worm all ready. Reno inspected the workmanship and found it perfect. The boiler was made from a fifty-gallon steel drum. One end of the drum had been removed entirely and a ten-inch hole cut out of the top of the drum. Inside the drum a heavy-gauge steel funnel had been rolled and welded into the drum to create a flue for flames to pass. The flue looked like an upside-down, extra-large steel funnel. On the top and center of the drum, the flue stuck out about six inches above the rim and acted as the flue exhaust. Also on the top was the original, three-inch screw cap. Across from the cap was a coupling welded into the top where a 1½-inch pipe would be threaded. On the side of the drum were two petcocks—one about a foot from the top of the drum and the other about two feet down on the same side beneath the first. These served as relief valves and could be used to check the water level in the drum.

The welds were precise and the workmanship excellent. The doubling keg was made from a twenty-five-gallon stainless steel drum. The top of the doubling keg had two 1½-inch couplings welded to it for inserting threaded pipes. The purifier was a small, fifteen-gallon wooden keg with two 1½-inch holes in the top for pipes. The worm was made of another fifty-gallon steel drum. Two ¾-inch holes were cut into it. One hole was close to the top on the side of the drum. The other was about eight inches from the bottom on the opposite side. From the holes protruded about six inches of ¾-inch copper pipe. The drum interior contained a massive copper coil. The coil was the condenser for cooling, also known as "the worm." We loaded "the giant" and all of its parts and returned to the store, parking in the back so nobody would notice us.

The moonshine whiskey still with boiler, cooker, doublin' keg, purifier, and worm

Setting Up for the Run

Reno and I sat in the truck and talked about what we needed in order to set up the giant. Again Reno rubbed his head and his face as he began ticking off what we needed. He tapped his palm with each item he announced.

"Let's see, Dino. We needs to load da barrels, meal, sugar, about ten cinder blocks, twenty foot of rubber hosing for the blow-out hose, some buckets, da burner and propane tanks. Oh yea, Dino. Grab a hoe foe mixing and I ah git sumtin' ta cover the barrels."

We got out of the truck and entered the back of the store and started to gather our items to load. We put our entire inventory by the large garage door at the back of the store and then opened the garage door and the back doors to the truck. We loaded the inventory onto the old Ford, closed the doors, and made sure we didn't leave anything behind. Reno drove the Ford out to the barn, and we loaded the four barrels. It was mid-morning, and we needed to get the truck contents to the site and unloaded. Before we got back into the truck, Reno told me to check the brake and signal lights. I stood behind the truck and watched as the brakes came on: each signal light worked.

"It all works, Reno!" I yelled up to him.

We climbed into the old Ford, eased out of the barnyard, and headed down Buffalo Road toward Wilson's Mills. My excitement couldn't have been stronger, although the prospect of being caught by the law was a real concern. We drove for several miles until we got close to where Percy's brother had once lived. Reno applied the brakes and the old truck ducked its front end and slightly swerved. We made a right turn and headed down a dirt path for about a quarter mile. The road led to a fishing pond. We stopped by a foxhound pen and pulled the truck into the edge of the woods where it was covered from the eyes of low-flying airplanes.

"It's right out there behind the dog pen. There's a natural spring. Water just comes up out the ground," Reno said.

How did he know that? I had lived around there forever and didn't know there was a natural spring out there in the woods. I'd never even seen a natural spring, didn't know such a thing existed. As we exited the truck we looked around and listened for other people or cars. Of course none should be there, but we couldn't be too careful. We unloaded the little giant and all the truck's contents and carried it behind the dog pen, placing it near the setup site. We carried each item for about 300 feet to the site. Reno explained that we had to carry the giant and be sure not to drag it; we didn't want to make a path for anybody to see.

The heavy propane tanks and the giant were heavy, and it was barely within my power to keep up with Reno. Even though I felt very strong from years of racing, Reno was hardcore strong and keeping up was difficult. My shirt was wet with sweat and the drops ran into my eyes and burned. I didn't know a boy could sweat like that. It was hard labor, but showing weakness or hcsitance was not an option. I was getting just what I had asked for. This was all business. Reno treated me just like any other man and expected me to keep up.

This was a rite of passage. At this point my childhood innocence left and I crossed over into manhood. The risks were real, and the work was backbreaking. Finally, we had the giant at the spring, and we made one last trip to check the area to make sure we hadn't left a trail or anything lying behind.

When we returned, Reno walked another thirty feet or so and said, "Dino, dar' it is, right dar'."

There was a hole in the ground, a natural spring, about six feet in diameter full of crystal clear water. There was no other water around, no creek or anything. *How could I have not known about this?* Then, giving myself some credit, I excused my lack of knowledge, as this was something no one else knew either. This was hidden from everyone in the woods in a place where no one would have any reason to be.

"Here, Dino, my boy," Reno said, magically producing two Pepsis, one for each of us. I never thought that far ahead and was glad he did. We sat on a five-gallon bucket and drank our sodas, discussing how we would set up the giant. The break was short.

"Now be quiet and listen and keep your eyes open, Dino. If you see the law just follow me and run." At this my senses were on red alert for anything that moved. We walked around the spring and pointed out where we would place the giant.

"Right dar, Dino. Put two cinder blocks right dar and three dar beside them ones. We'll set the boiler up dar and the cooker right side it, not far from the water."

I took two blocks and placed them about eighteen inches apart so that the fifty-gallon boiler would sit on them. Next we carried the boiler over and placed it on the blocks and sat the cooker on the three blocks beside the boiler. We took the time to shore it up so that it sat straight up and was solid feeling. We connected a 1½-inch steel pipe to the top of the boiler and elbowed it down to the base of the cooker. A pipe extended from the base of the cooker inlet. We connected the two with a union using a pipe wrench. In front and to the right of the cooker we set the stainless steel doubling keg on two blocks. From the top of the cooker cap I ran a 1½-inch pipe over to the keg and again connected the two with a union joint and pipe wrench. There was also a shutoff valve between the cooker and the doubling keg. To the right of the doubling keg we sat the wooden purifier on one block.

Next, we placed two blocks to the right of the purifier, and Reno said, "That looks 'bout right, Dino." We placed the fifty-gallon worm, or condenser, on those two blocks. We connected the purifier and worm in a similar manner, completing the setup. At the left of the boiler we placed two hundred-pound propane tanks and set the burner underneath the boiler.

The little giant was ready to go to work. It was a perfect piece of work. Even Reno thought so.

"Dino, let's set the barrels over here." We carried the barrels to a spot about ten feet from the cooker.

"Dino, we needs to cook the mash, my boy," Reno told me.

Mixing the mash ingredients was one of the keys to making successful whiskey. According to the 1958 *Saturday Evening Post*, it was Percy's recipe and his method of distilling the mash—and of course the large quantities—that made him notorious and distinguished him as the king of the moonshiners. His secret was a well-guarded one that I was able to learn and keep. Everybody who knew whiskey knew that Percy's was the best and the smoothest. His hooch was shipped up and down the Eastern seaboard and as far west as California. The smoothness of a whiskey was what made it a good sipping whiskey, void of hardness and bitterness.

Mixing the Mash

Many moonshiners had their own mash mix. For the little giant, we used a simple mix of corn meal, barley and hops, sugar, and a little yeast. Dino told me we needed some hot water to cook the meal so we ought to get the boiler going. "Dino, get ah bucket and some water and bring it over here. Ya need to open the boiler cap and pour it full of water."

I took a white five-gallon bucket and walked over to the natural spring, bent down to the water, and dipped the bucket into it, watching the crystal clear water fill the bucket about two-thirds full. I carried the bucket to the boiler and sat it down. Reno was maneuvering a hundred-pound propane tank nearer the boiler. I easily and quietly removed the cap from the boiler, careful not to tap the drum with the wrench and make a loud noise: steel against steel would echo through the woods. The cap had a rubber gasket on it. I laid the cap and gasket on the top of the boiler and carefully poured the water into the boiler without spilling it. Some water did spill down the side of the boiler and made a small puddle on the ground.

It took ten trips to the spring to finally fill the boiler. By the last bucket of water, my arms shook and I struggled to lift the bucket up high enough to pour the water into the boiler. The top of the boiler was soaked and the ground around the boiler was a little wet from where the water had run over the side. Reno was finishing the propane tank and burner hookup. Water leaked from the petcock located on the side of the boiler. After closing the petcock, I replaced the cap and gasket onto the boiler and then tightened the cap with a pair of channel locks. Reno called me over.

"Dino, look down here. This is the burner, and this is how ya set up under here. Now, when this thang lights off it ah sounds like a little train roaring. Let's light it and heat up da water. Ya better let me light it. I don't want you to get blowed up, my boy." Reno opened the gas valve on the top of the hundred-pound tank. We could hear the propane hissing from the burner. There were no safety valves or precautions using the burner. You just had to be careful. He quickly struck at the first wooden match.

"Heck fire, Dino. Watch out!"

He quickly struck a second and tossed it, the end of the match burning with excitement. The match landed under the boiler and a loud *ka-poof* bellowed out of the top of the boiler flue's exhaust. Reno took a step toward the propane tank to open the valve. The boiler began to roar, and some sparks shot out of the top. Reno was satisfied.

"Listen to dat, Dino. We'll have some hot water in a few minutes," he said.

Exhaust began to billow from the boiler. It looked like the smoke from a large tractor muffler. The limbs and leaves above were blowing and tossing over the boiler as it heated the water.

"Dino, get the meal and brang it to the barrels."

I carried the bags of meal and set them by the barrels.

"Now, this is how we make the mash, Dino. Take my knife and open that bag and pour half of it in the barrel and d'other half in dat barrel. I git d' other bag."

Reno asked for his knife. He opened the other bag of meal so we could pour half into each barrel. The meal poured into the charred barrels, covering their bottoms while little puffs of corn dust floated up.

"Now, Dino, don't forget to keep watching out for the law," Reno reminded.

He walked over and placed his hand on the cooker. "It won't be long now and dis little giant will be jumping."

A few minutes later, a small amount of steam began to ease out of the worm's end. Reno walked over, concerned, and looked into the fifty-gallon worm barrel.

"Dino, you ain't got no water in the worm barrel. Good gracious, boy, yuh gots to put water in the worm barrel."

Shit, I ain't had time to fart, much less put water in the worm barrel. I hurried over and began making more trips to the spring with the five-gallon bucket to fill the worm barrel and please Reno. As the water filled the worm barrel up to the coiled copper, the steam turned to water and began to run in a steady flow. Reno was now more concerned.

"Look at dat. Steam's coming out. We'll lose whiskey like dat."

Steam hissed out of a small crack where the steel pipe entered into the wooden keg purifier. "Dino, swedge it up."

"What? What swedging mean?" I asked.

"You don't know how to swedge?" Reno said. "Good gracious, Dino. I gots to learn you some thangs. Get a piece of that old rag over there."

There was an old piece of cloth by the barrel that looked like an old t-shirt. I took the cloth to Reno and he cut a small piece.

Using a stick, he began pushing the cloth into the slight crack where the steam was escaping. There were a couple of other slight steam leaks around the barrel as well.

Reno took a handful of meal, mixed it with water, slapped it in the cracks, and said, "When dat barrel gets wet it uh swell and seal up."

OK, if you say so. Reno directed me to get the large blowout hose connected to the cooker's base and put the end into one of the barrels. He walked over to the barrel and held the blowout hose.

"Now, Dino, go over and open the blowout valve on the bottom of the cooker," he instructed.

I did what he said and felt the rubberized blowout hose begin to get hot.

"Now, Dino, close dat valve 'tween the cooker and doubling keg and do it right slow like."

When I closed the valve, the blowout hose began to dance on the ground. Reno wrestled the hose into the first barrel as hot water began to fill the barrel. He quickly maneuvered the hot hose from one barrel to the next putting just the right amount of water in each one to cook the meal.

"Dat's enough. Open da cooker valve and close the blowout valve, Dino."

The water stopped flowing out of the blowout hose and the worm began to flow again. Reno walked over and turned the propane tank valve counter-clockwise to close the flow of propane to the massive burner. The limbs and leaves stopped shaking, and it became calm and quiet again in the woods. We looked around and listened for a minute or so.

Reno broke the quiet, whispering, "Get the hoe." He used the hoe to lightly mix the hot water into the corn meal in the barrels, forming it into corn dough.

"Now we gone cook it for a few minutes."

After a few minutes, Reno relit the boiler burner and I became master of the valves as we forced the rest of the boiler water through the cooker and into the barrels.

"Dino, start branging some water and filling up the barrels."

My trips to the spring continued for a while until the each barrel was about one-third full of water.

"Get the hoe, Dino." Reno began breaking up the corn meal that had cooked itself together. As he mashed it with the hoe large and small pieces of the meal began floating up. We used our hands and reached into the barrels to separate the clods of meal. It felt just like when Mama made cornmeal for corn bread.

The water was still warm, and Reno told me to get the sugar. I opened the bags of sugar and began to pour the white crystals into the mash mix as Reno used the hoe to mix and melt it with the corn meal and water. We did the same for every barrel. We also added a bit of hops after the sugar. As Reno continued to mix the mash I returned to the spring and toted buckets of water, two at a time, to fill the barrels close to full.

Carrying the buckets of water was a struggle. Having a water pump or water hose would surely have been helpful.

This is a lot of work. I was soaked in sweat, and it was a cool day.

Finally the barrels were near full. We checked each one to ensure the mash was mixed well. Reno pulled out a small package of yeast.

"This ah help it start to work a little faster, but if you ain't got none it ah still work off."

He sprinkled a little of the yeast over the top of the sweetened mash. We tasted the mash before covering the tops and it was sweet and actually tasted good. We used some matting and covered the tops of the barrels to keep animals, leaves, and debris out. Before leaving, we gathered some branches and covered our little giant and the barrels to conceal them.

"Dino, make sure dar ain't nothin' laying around and let's go." I looked around the giant, and it was clean.

Now that the work was ending, it occurred to us that the law might be hiding in the woods and ready to rush in and capture us. I took special care when looking at the giant to survey the woods for law officers. It was getting dark as the sun was going down and it was difficult to see into the woods. The shadows were vague, but my imagination was specific. The more I looked, the more it looked like someone was there.

Reno was making his way toward the dog pen in a slow walk. He was carefully watching for anything unusual. As we walked out of the woods it felt like we were squirrel hunting, except this time we were watching for the law. The night was cool, calm, and completely quiet except for the sound of bugs and mosquitoes. Even though we were careful and tried to be quiet, I could hear our steps through the weeds and grass. It was so dark that every shadowy shape in my view seemed to a be a law man.

We made it to the old Ford and quietly opened the doors and climbed in. The truck's door squeaked again, but this time it sounded a hundred times louder. I opened it just enough to slide in. Reno patted the accelerator, and I cringed as the big Ford motor turned over several times before starting. We had broken the quiet of the night and were now exposed to anyone within hearing distance. The old Ford rumbled up the dirt path with the lights off, and we made our way onto the paved road toward the store. As we pulled onto the paved road Reno turned on the headlights.

"What yu thank, Dino?"

The First Run

About five days later, Reno was sitting at the store when I walked in.

"Dino, my boy, we needs to take a little trip."

OK.

We walked through the store and exited out the back where his old maroon Ford Fairlane was parked.

"We needs to check the barrels and sees if they ready," he whispered. I liked Reno's car. It was a four-door, automatic transmission, with a chrome searchlight mounted by the driver's vent window, just like a police car. It had heavier shocks and springs to carry heavy loads. Also on the back were mud grips. Mud grips looked cool on a car because they were usually just on trucks. I was excited about the mash as we headed toward the little giant. Driving down the dirt path, we stopped the car about 400 feet from the dog pen and backed it up into a small cutaway area in the woods. The area was just big enough for the car. The car was just about completely concealed from the path by overhanging tree branches.

"Now, Dino, stay quiet and watch out for da law. We gone walk in from behind da pen, so look out and be quiet," Reno said softly.

Slightly hunched over, we walked cautiously through the woods and listened. As we approached the little giant, we could see that everything looked the way we'd left it. We stopped short about a hundred feet and just watched for about two minutes. Then we cautiously moved toward the giant and stopped by the barrels. Reno slowly removed the top from the first barrel and we peeked in. There were hundreds of small gnats flying around the mash and more came flying out when Reno lifted the top. The mash looked a little milky, and an occasional bubble popped out. Reno told me to lean over and take in a big breath and see what it smelled like. I did and then jumped back as it felt like my nose was going to burn off of my face. I felt light-headed.

Reno smiled. "It must be 'bout ready, Dino." We lifted the tops to the other barrels just enough to peer inside and make sure they were ready too. We covered the first barrel back up and made our way back to the car. As we rode to the store, Reno said the mash was almost ready and we needed to "run it" within the next few days or it would sour. We decided on the day after next.

That day I went to the store early in the morning and met Reno. We went to the kitchen, and he cooked some eggs and bacon. He cooked the bacon especially for me because he didn't eat pork. He said the Bible said not to eat a hoof-footed animal. Anyways, Reno cooked eggs and bacon over the old black stove and made some biscuits. He put the eggs on paper plates. Up in the cabinet was Karo syrup.

"Dino, dis is what you like, my boy." He pulled the bottle of syrup from the cabinet and set it by my plate. The syrup had dripped down the side of the bottle from earlier use, making the bottle sticky. Reno poured the syrup on my plate for the biscuits. He smiled as he poured it because he knew it was one of my favorites. I smiled back and ate.

Percy came in the kitchen as we were eating and said, "Perry, you mean you gonna eat here, nasty as this kitchen is? Howard, you ought not keep this place so damn nasty. You won't catch me eaten outta here."

Percy was just joking with Reno because I'd seen him eat out of that kitchen many a time before. Percy and I even cut pork shoulders using the band saw by the door. Percy would switch on the large vertical band saw and the blade would make a high-pitched *ummmmmmm* sound as it cut through the shoulder bone. White stuff seeped out of the meat as the saw eased its way through the bone. Percy would make several slices to fix us ham and eggs. So I knew he liked to eat out of that "nasty" kitchen.

When breakfast was over, Percy asked, "Reno, you and Perry gonna go down there this morning?"

Reno nodded.

"Well, be careful and don't get your asses caught now."

We finished breakfast and walked to the back of the store. Reno ticked off a list of supplies we would need. "Dino, we needs fo' cases of jars and some mo' sugar and a funnel and a couple of clean buckets and a clean white sheet."

The cases of jars were in another room beside John D's room. Each case had four one-gallon glass jars. Each jar had a thumb ring for picking it up. Four cases equaled sixteen gallons. I pulled the cases out from beside the wall and set them by the door. Reno came up with the sheet.

"We gots two hundred pounds of sugar and two clean five-gallon buckets," he noted. Then he backed his car up to the garage door. I heard the motor shut off and that was my cue to open the big garage door. I unlatched the door lock and pulled with all my might to raise the door. As the door began to open, the cool morning air rushed into the garage and reminded me of just how cool it was that day.

We loaded everything in the boot and back seat. We got into the car and Reno started the engine and turned on the heater.

He rubbed his hands together and said, "Yes sar, Dino, it's cool today, but we ah be all right."

Reno reached down and pulled up a brown paper sack that he had already loaded into the car. "Look here, my boy. Bet you didn't thank about this," he said. In the sack he had orange nabs, four Pepsis, and four sweet potatoes wrapped in aluminum foil. He had grown the sweet potatoes himself and was proud to show me that he'd brought them just for us.

"We's ah put deez on the boiler, cook um, put ah little butter on um and it'a be sumtheng good. What ya thank about that, my boy?"

Thanks, Reno. He was unusually spirited that day, like a child on Christmas morning. It was the opportunity to run the little giant that excited him. The years of mass whiskey making were long gone for Percy and Reno. We headed toward the woods as the car sputtered a little from the cold. Reno patted the accelerator several times to keep the car from stalling. In just a few minutes the heater was putting out warm air, and I lowered my hands down by the vents to warm them. It was still early, and no other cars were on the roads. Back then, there weren't many cars out anyway, much less early in the morning.

We made the right turn down the dirt path and drove to the dog pen. Reno carefully pulled the car off the path and looked all around us for anything unusual. Again the cool morning air made me wish for a warmer morning. We opened the back doors and removed a couple cases of jars and placed them under the tree. We opened the boot and removed the rest of our items, leaving them by the tree while we slipped down to the giant.

"Let's make sure ever'thang is all right before we go down there with all this," he said.

We slipped behind the dog pen and surveyed the area by the natural spring and the little giant. It all looked undisturbed since our last visit. Reno said he would move the car back to the hiding place and I could start carrying the jars and sugar to the giant. As he pulled up the path and the car disappeared, I felt a little alone and noticed the still quiet of the morning more than before. Carrying the cases to the site, I could hear every step and noticed my shoes getting a little wet from the morning dew on the weeds and tall grass. Walking past a low-bending limb, I walked through a spider web that stuck to my face and hair. I brushed it away and continued, hoping that the spider wasn't on me. It was a slight relief to know that nobody had gone down this route lately or they would have run into the web.

By the time Reno came up, I had managed to get all the items to the giant. Even though I was looking for him, he had slipped unnervingly close before I saw him. Good thing he wasn't the law. Under his arm he carried the bag of food with the Pepsis. It was nice to see he'd remembered, as I was already thirsty. The smell of the mash was strong even from a distance. We pulled the covers off of the barrels and observed the mash. It was mostly clear with an occasional bubble floating to the top. Reno told me to fill the boiler as he removed the cooker cap with a wrench. I made the usual multiple trips to the spring with the two five-gallon buckets and began to fill the boiler. This time I used the funnel that we had brought with us. When the water began to run from the petcock, I closed it and added a couple more gallons of water to top it off. I walked over to the open top cooker and looked in it. With the top off, the opening was about ten inches in diameter and easy to see into.

"Dino, brang ya buckets over here," Reno called as I approached the barrels of mash.

"Now what ya wants to do is scoop dis mash out easy-like, cause the meal has settled to the bottom and we don't wants the meal in the cooker."

Reno eased the bucket in the mash barrel to show me how to scoop the mash out without disturbing the settled meal. He carried the mash over to the cooker and poured it in. He handed me the bucket and told me to fill the cooker just about full. Reno went over to the boiler and lit the large burner. The boiler roared to life again, shaking the limbs above the flue exhaust as the high-pressure exhaust rushed up through the trees. Most of the leaves were gone from the last time we'd lit it. Listening to the boiler roar, I dipped the bucket into the mash barrel and began filling the cooker.

The smell of alcohol was strong and steamed up in my face each time I scooped a bucket of the mash up. The more I scooped, the more I had to lean into the barrel to reach the mash. Toward the bottom of the barrel the corn meal began to swirl as I tried to scoop the last of the mash out. One barrel of mash filled the little giant's cooker perfectly, as if it had been made just for this purpose. The mash was about eight inches from the top of the cooker neck.

Reno inspected my work, and I began to put the top back onto the cooker, tightening all eight bolts snugly. The steel pipe extending from the cooker top matched perfectly with the doubling keg inlet pipe. All that was left was to pull the two pipes together and connect the union with a pipe wrench.

"Dino, make sure that the valve's open or it'll blow up," Reno advised. I inspected the lever valve between the cooker and the doubling keg; it was definitely open so it would not explode.

"Now, Dino, this is a little steam giant perfect for brandy, but it'uh run whiskey alright too. Dat burner will make steam from that boiler and it runs right down here in this pipe in da bottom of da cooker. Da steam ah brang da mash to a boil and steam out da whiskey. The alcohol will go out of this pipe from da cooker into the doublin' keg and outa the doublin' keg by dis pipe into da purifier and den to da worm, and da whiskey will come out here. You gots to be sure you keep da water in the worm barrel cold or you ah lose the whiskey cause it'a steam out."

Reno pointed to each pipe as he explained the operation. Seemed simple enough, but Percy had already drawn it out for me on a brown paper sack and shown me how it should work.

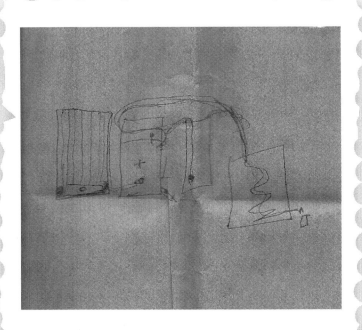

A rough sketch of the still's mechanics and operation drawn by Percy Flowers on the back of a paper bag from Flowers Store

"Now, my boy, we will have us something good in a while," Reno said. He took the four sweet potatoes wrapped in aluminum foil and placed them on the top of the boiler by the flue exit. We smiled at each other. Then he made a motion with his hand for me to follow him. We walked over to the two clean buckets and moved them to a spot by themselves near the worm. We placed the white sheet in one bucket, careful not to get it dirty, and put the other bucket under the copper worm outlet. In about fifteen minutes, the little giant began to shake and rock on the cinder blocks.

Reno leaned down and smelled the copper worm outlet. "It won't be long now, Dino."

The little giant kept shaking, and in a few minutes a little steam puffed out the end of the copper worm outlet. A few moments later, a small stream of whiskey began to run out into the bucket. Reno ran his finger through the steady stream of whiskey and held it up, smelled it, and touched his tongue. "Now, Dino, try dat."

Leaning down, I put my index finger in the stream of whiskey. At this moment I was baptized in my own Southern whiskey from my very own giant. I smelled the strong alcohol on my finger and touched it to my tongue. It was strong and pure moonshine.

Reno just smiled. "Dat's it, my boy!"

The whiskey stream began to increase, and a little steam puffed out again.

"Goot gracious, it's getting too hot," Reno said. He went to the propane tank and turned the gas valve down a little to lower the burner fire and heat. The whiskey stream slowed, and the water in the worm barrel began to steam out a little. The water was becoming too hot.

"Dino, you getting' behind on dat worm barrel. You got to bucket dat water out and keep cold water in it or we gonna lose the whiskey."

The next hour was pure hell. It took all my might to keep the hot water scooped out of the barrel and fresh cold water in it. As fast as I could scoop it out and put cold water in, it was hot again. I sweated like a person who'd just ran a mile with pneumonia. Finally Reno motioned me over to the worm.

"Now, Dino, these are the backins. The first dat comes out is pure alcohol. You can't drank it like dat. It'a burn you up. We gone filter it and mix it to sipping whiskey."

First we had to blow the mash out of the cooker and back into the barrel. Reno grabbed the big blowout hose and held it in the barrel that we had earlier emptied into the cooker. "Dino, open the blowout valve and close da doubling keg valve."

I did exactly as he instructed, and the blowout hose began to buck like an angry snake as Reno held it into the barrel. The contents of the cooker was forced through the blowout hose by the boiler steam, refilling the mash barrel with hot water and the remnants of the previous mash. The blowout hose made a loud *hissss* and steam bellowed out. The angry snakelike hose then settled back down, and Reno motioned to reverse the valves. I opened the doubling keg valve and closed the cooker blowout valve to direct the steam out of the worm. Reno turned the propane tank valve off, and the angry fire-breathing burner went out. The calm of the still morning returned. As the boiler cooled, it made an occasional pop like the hot exhaust of a cooling motorcycle engine.

"Dino, get da sugar and pour it in here." Reno pointed to the barrel that we'd just filled with hot water. We opened the bag and poured the sugar into the barrel and Reno mixed it with the hoe.

"You don't need no mo' meal. Dis'll work off again before we have to add some," he explained. We stirred and mixed the sugar with the meal, added hops and a little yeast, and put the cover on the barrel for it to start fermenting again. We walked over to the bucket of whiskey sitting by the worm outlet. The bucket was about two-thirds full. A third bucket, half full, sat by the side, and the other bucket still sat with the white sheet in it. Reno explained that he had poured the straight whiskey, about the first two gallons, into a separate bucket and that we had to "cut it" for sipping whiskey—dilute it with the bucket of "backins" or less-pure whiskey. Both buckets looked completely crystal clear to me, but Reno said we needed to strain it through the sheet.

Reno pulled out his knife and handed it to me. "Dino, cut me a piece dat's just big anuf ta fit over dat bucket." We placed the small sheet over the clean empty bucket. Reno told me to hold the sheet as he poured the two gallons of pure whiskey through the white sheet. It took a while for it to filter through and sometimes got close to the top of the sheet and Reno had to slow down the pouring to allow it time to filter in.

"In the big giants we used special sand filters," he said, referring to the old days of moonshining. We filtered about a gallon of the backins through the filter, and then he swirled the whiskey around to mix it up good.

"Dino, git me a jar and hold dis funnel up in it."

I put one of the gallon jars down near him and placed the funnel in the top. Reno poured about a half gallon of the mixed whiskey into the funnel and jar and then screwed the top on it. He held the jar up and shook it a couple of times. All the shaking created large bubbles that lingered at the top of the jar.

Reno opened the jar and placed it to his lips and took a sip. "Whuuu, Dinnooo, dat's too strong."

That was the first time I had ever seen Reno taste any spirits. He never drank. He placed the jar on the ground and we continued mixing the backins and testing the strength until Reno was satisfied. We ended up with exactly four one-gallon glass jars of perfect whiskey from that first barrel of mash. Percy was right when he predicted that we would get about four gallons to the barrel. We did exactly.

When Reno said it was just right for sipping, he encouraged me to try it. It seemed too strong, but I never liked to drink whiskey or beer. I had waited as long as I could remember to learn how to make whiskey from Percy, and now I held the recipe in my hands and etched it into my memory forever. Reno showed me how to test the whiskey and mix it for sipping. He also showed me that the straight whiskey would burn a blue flame if you put fire to it. For a moment I forgot about the law and the possibility of getting caught. We were very pleased with our first run of moonshine.

We had three barrels still to run. Reno directed me to get cold water in the worm barrel so we could run the other mash. Over the next several hours, we worked hard firing the boiler, running the mash, and resetting the barrels for the next run. It was evening when we finished. We had a total of sixteen gallons of perfect Southern sippin' whiskey made from Percy's own recipe. Reno and I sat the cases by the edge of the barrels where we began our walk out toward the dog pen. We looked around the area and picked up all of our trash and put it into a bag. We each picked up a case of the whiskey and quietly slipped through the woods and placed the cases behind the dog pen. We had two cases to go.

Reno told me to get the other cases and he would get the car. At that moment, we heard walkie-talkie chatter coming from up the path. Reno grabbed me and pulled me down low as we slipped back behind the dog pen. We hunkered down and sat completely still. My heart beat wildly, throbbing in my ear. Reno looked at me with the most serious face I can remember ever seeing on him. We listened intently as the voices became clearer over the walkie-talkie. We had a view of the path, but the daylight was almost gone. I kept watch mostly behind us as Reno watched the front toward the path. It was now very difficult to see into the woods, especially to make out a person.

Reno pulled on my arm with one hand and put his finger over his lips with the other to say, *be really quiet.* He slowly pointed through the limbs and weeds toward the path. A woman was riding a horse down the path. We waited for about a half hour more before we eased our way out of the woods. There were several horse tracks on the road. Reno guessed that it was not the law. By now, my senses allowed me to recognize the coldness from my sweat-covered shirt. It was cold, not cool. Reno told me again that he would get the car and I should get the other two cases.

I looked back into the woods and felt real fear. They now seemed scary. I could not show any weakness and reasoned in my mind that there couldn't be anything out there anyway. Reno slipped back into the woods toward the giant and I followed closely behind. He headed up the woods several hundred feet and I returned to get the remaining two cases. I carried the first case to the others by the dog pen and turned to go back for the forth. By now, it was completely dark, but the moon was bright and my eyes had adjusted to the dark. Going back into the woods was scary. I moved slowly and very carefully, scaring myself more with each step as I thought about ghosts and all the old ghost tales that folks used to talk about.

Carrying the last case, my steps back to the dog pen were much faster and my heart raced from fright. It felt like I was being followed, but of course it was my wild imagination. Reno's car came down the path as I eased out. He kept the lights off and drove it in the dark down the path. He backed up toward the pen and got out and opened the boot with his key. We loaded the whiskey in the boot and got back into the car. As we drove up the path, the moon lit our way and Reno kept the lights off. We reached the paved road and looked for cars coming. There were none.

Reno eased onto the road, turned the headlights on, and we made our way to the store. About halfway there, the car motor had warmed up and Reno turned the heat on. I was exhausted and also excited about our day.

As we approached the stop sign on Highway 42, we could see the store just across the road. Reno slowly drove past the west side of the store and entered the driveway where nobody could see us drive behind the store. The old car squeaked as Reno drove it through the potholes. We parked the car and entered the back of the store. We walked up to a set of doors that separated the back garage area from the customers and cracked the door to look in. Percy was sitting on a chair watching the TV. Reno cracked the door a little more, and Percy looked over. He got up and came to the back of the store.

"How is it?" Percy asked.

Reno had brought in a gallon to show him. Percy cracked the door again to see that nobody was in the store but Curry, who was standing by the register at the front entrance. Reno hid the gallon under his shirt, and we all made our way to the kitchen. Reno placed the gallon on the table, and it glistened in the light. Percy picked up the gallon and shook it as he looked at it. He opened the gallon and took a sip.

"Now dat's good, dat's made right. Well, Perry, looks like you know what ta do now. Just don't get your ass caught." I was thrilled that the great moonshine king himself had given his seal of approval on our first run.

I didn't realize it then, but making whiskey was already an old-school trade that had long before outlived its usefulness for moonshiners and bootleggers as a way of life. Little did I know that what I had just learned would soon be the last act of moonshining for the notorious moonshining kingpin Percy Flowers. He had handed me his secret to keep as though he were putting a good book on the shelf for the last time.

Percy's direct words to me as a father, for me to be a veterinarian or something more, were well intended and derived from many years of run-ins with the law. He wanted something better for me. Likewise, that is what I want for you boys.

All parents want better for their children than they themselves had. But wisdom grows mostly from experience. Many young people have to make their own mistakes, even if their

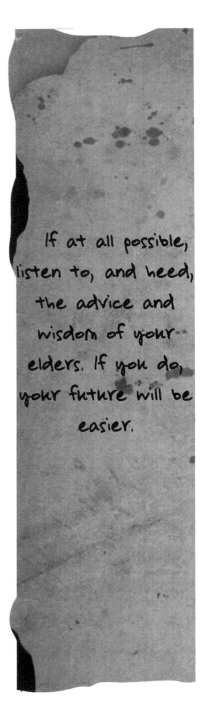

If at all possible, listen to, and heed, the advice and wisdom of your elders. If you do, your future will be easier.

parents cautioned them about the right way to go. There is a reason why older people are usually more wise: when you go through life, you can review and learn from your mistakes and see more clearly the path ahead, applying the lessons learned along the way. I was hardheaded, so the path of knowledge and learning has been a bit longer for me than for some others. I hope your path will be smoother and easier than mine. It is my hope that you boys will listen to wise men, not fools. If you do, your future will be easier.

11

MAKING MONEY

Dear Josh and John,

The objective of moonshining was to turn cornmeal and sugar into big money. Many folks allegedly made millions and built empires—one dollar at a time—selling illegal whiskey during Prohibition.

Percy was at the top of this list. He started with nothing, and during his lifetime he made millions and built an empire from the whiskey business. He was a shrewd businessman and invested in land, lots of it. His farms totaled approximately four to five thousand acres. Tenant farmers grew corn, tobacco, cotton, and soybeans, and these crops subsidized his earnings. Percy's land was known as some of the best in North Carolina. His moonshining fortune financed his appetite for foxhound racing and cockfighting.

Percy was an expert breeder and was known to have the best foxhounds in the world. Some hounds cost several thousand dollars each and at times he kept some two hundred of them on hand. Keep in mind that during the 1960s this was a great deal of money to spend on a dog. Percy's champion fighting cocks were also among the best and gained the well-deserved reputation as being unbeatable in the cockfighting underworld of big money men. At one time, Percy bet $10,000 on a single fight that lasted less than five seconds. He told me that he owned dozens of new Cadillacs over the years and countless trucks and other fast cars, many modified for maximum power and speed.

Percy was known as a millionaire and high roller, but he was as honest as any ordinary working man and always true to his word. Even an enemy would speak highly of his integrity. He always wore a brim hat, dressed well, and kept a cigar between his teeth to chew on when he was not smoking it. Money men stuck together. They had worked their way into the high rollers' club and they helped each other. It was a time when "men were men." They exuded complete confidence in themselves and "wishy-washy" was for punks. They weren't known for jogging, sipping coffee, taking a bike ride, or being diplomatically or politically correct. They didn't wear sneakers or shorts. Their ways were as hard as the times they came up in. When they said something, it was right and not to be questioned because they really did know what was right and wrong, what would work or not work. Their ways had earned men like that millions and that was, as they say, "the proof of the pudding." I wanted to be just like Percy and earn millions of my own, on my own.

Making whiskey was exciting and risky, and over time, my moonshining activities began to pay off. The morning after Reno and I had completed our first batch, I went to the store to see Reno. When he saw me, he motioned to me to come to the kitchen. He'd gotten there early and had already brought a couple of gallons of the whiskey to the kitchen and set them on the table. The gallons were wrapped in brown paper sacks. That morning we cooked more than breakfast. We cooked sugar.

While we made scrambled eggs and bacon the large pot on the big burner was cooking pure cane sugar. I stirred the thick, golden-looking sugar occasionally to keep it from burning. After breakfast, Reno opened a gallon of clear whiskey and we poured it into two half-gallon jars, leaving each a couple of inches from being full. The mouth of the half-gallon glass jars were large, about three inches in diameter, which made them easy to work with. We took a ladle full of the hot cooked sugar out of the pot and added it to the half-gallon jars. The whiskey turned dark golden. We then poured the half gallons into pint jars. We finished and even cleaned up the kitchen.

Later in the day, Reno told me to come on; he said that we were going to Sutie Bell and Brar Hopper's house. Sutie ran the liquor house in Red Hill, a community of Negros just a few miles from the store.

I had been to Sutie and Brar Hopper's house several times over the years but didn't know why. Most of the time, she would motion us in. One time as a boy, we went to Sutie's for a quick visit and she said, "Perry, how my baby doing?" She always said that to me when I went there. She called me her baby.

One time she hobbled over to her bed and sat down. As she sat on the bed, it bent in the middle from her weight and nearly touched the floor. She motioned for me to come sit by her. She placed her large flabby arm over my shoulder. It was jellylike and heavy. I naturally leaned against her from the bed bending in the middle. She just talked and told me how good it was to see me again. That was a normal visit to Sutie's.

Brar Hopper was known for working on chain saws and cutting wood. His left hand bent down ninety degrees—a permanent disfigurement from an old gunshot to the wrist. However, his deformed hand didn't slow him up any in working. Brar Hopper also came over to our house to help cut wood, and he repaired my minibike when it needed it. Brar often stuttered, but I could understand him just fine. Even though Brar was the man of the house, there was no doubt who ruled the roost. If Brar got out of line, Sutie would take care of him. Nobody messed with Sutie. She would cut or shoot the shit out of anyone, and Brar was no exception. He just had more opportunity since he and Sutie lived together.

We pulled into the dirt driveway right up to the front steps. The entire side yard was dirt where so many people had parked in the yard. I saw Reno looking around for other cars and people before we got out. We opened the large boot of Reno's Ford. It seemed huge and strangely empty but for a couple of gallons of whiskey, wrapped in brown paper sacks, sitting in a box. Reno took a gallon and we went up the cracked steps onto the worn wooden porch, a structure that was mostly void of paint as it had been worn off over the years.

Sutie had heard us drive up and stood peeking through the cracked-open screen door. I noticed her large, flower-patterned dress and thought to myself, *she sure is a big woman.* Sutie opened the door, and we went in.

"How you today, Miss Sutie?" Reno asked with a smile.

"You know I good, and how's my baby, Perry?" She smiled. "Perry, how you been? I ain't seen you in a *ll-looonnnng* time. Your mama doin' good, baby?"

"Yep, she's good," I said.

Reno placed the gallon of whiskey on the kitchen table. She edged over to the table and pulled the gallon jar out of the brown paper sack and placed it back on the table where it was in clear view. Just over by the sink was a small stack of Dixie Cups. Sutie hobbled over to the cups and took one from the stack. She placed the cup on the table, opened the gallon of whiskey, and poured about an ounce of whiskey and tasted it.

"Un huh, dat alright!" She placed the cup back on the table. She reached into the top of her dress, fumbled with her brassiere, and pulled out a roll of money secured with a rubber band around it. Surprised at where she kept her money, I wondered how much she had in there. I'd heard that women kept money in their bras, but I'd never seen it before. As she counted out the money, I turned my head. I didn't want her to think I was staring, although I was so surprised at her hiding place that I guess I was.

"Thank you, Miss Sutie," Reno said. He pulled his wallet from his pants pocket and placed the money in his large bifold wallet. I noticed the chrome chain that secured it to his belt.

"When ya comin' back?" she asked Reno as she put the rolled-up money back into place.

"Oh, I come back when ya want me to," Reno replied with a smile.

"Well come on back in 'bout three days. Perry, you take care yo'self, baby," she called.

I waved bye, and we went back to the store.

In just a few weeks of making and selling moonshine, a person could make several hundred dollars. For a seventeen-year-old country boy that was a lot of money and a significant temptation. By comparison, Curry earned just three hundred dollars a month as a grocery store clerk and that was after working thirty years. In that area, money was hard to come by and so were good jobs. I felt that I was on my way to walking in Percy's shoes. Little did I know that the days of making millions in the whiskey business were long gone and that I was only getting a taste of what it had been like so long before.

I was, in a sense, making hay while the sun was shining. Or making whiskey while the moon was shining. But the point is, I was making lots of money and didn't realize that the end to my days of moonshining was coming horribly quickly and with devastating consequences.

12

THE WORST DAY OF PERCY'S LIFE

Dear Josh and John,

Everyone has a best and worst day in his or her life. I've had quite a few bad days—and a lot of good ones. Bringing a child into the world is a "best day" for most people, and losing a child is for parents, the worst day of a parent's life. As for Percy, he had many good days, but his worst day was one that haunted him forever. That was the day his son Percy Jr. was killed—a day that he painfully recalled to me as we sat on the old, white "bench of knowledge."

It was a day no different than any other sitting on the old white bench in front of the store. The doors to the store were open to allow cool air into the store. Curry leaned against the doorframe, listening as I asked Percy one question after another. Curry stepped out onto the sidewalk.

"Perry, stop talking so much. You're just a question box," he mumbled, stepping back into the store to tend the register.

After he stepped back inside, I decided to venture onto a sensitive subject about which I knew little and Percy had said even less. I asked Percy about his son Percy Jr. and how he had died in an airplane crash. After the accident, the carcass of the plane was moved into the woods and sat deserted. As it turned out, Percy was going to tell me a story I'd rather not have heard.

Percy sat quiet for a few moments with his forearms resting on his knees and his head held down. Then he slowly looked over at me, and I could see through his smudged, metal-rim glasses that his eyes squinted a little and were watery. But his voice was firm. He looked at me sternly—in a way he'd never done before.

"Perry, now I want you to forget about them airplanes. Them damn things will kill you. Jimmy broke his neck in one, lucky it didn't kill him. That damn airplane killed Percy Jr., and that was the worst day of my life. I didn't even want to see that plane, so I had Billy and Jimmy move it. They put that thang in the woods behind Jimmy's store. Perry, I sure hope you never have to go through something like that. It like to kill me."

"What happened that killed him?" I asked.

202

"The motor quit after he took off, and he landed in a ditch," Percy said grimly. And then he paused for a moment.

"The motor was forced back to where he was sitting and just killed him. He left two little boys. Their mama took them and raised them. It was sure the worst day of my life. Now, don't you fuck around with them airplanes 'cause I don't want you to get hurt. I never want to go through that again."

I had heard about Percy Jr. from Mama several times. She said that Percy Jr. was a handsome man. Mama said that he took after his mama, Delma's, side of the family. She was a beautiful woman. Mama said he was more than good looking, he was a good man, kind and considerate to all the folks around there. He was going to law school to be a lawyer. She said that Percy worked his son hard on the farm. A man was meant to work hard, in Percy's view, in order to become something in life.

Percy Jr. had a passion for flying. He bought an old experimental Ryan airplane from World War II. Mama said he would fly right over the fields so low you could see him in the cockpit.

"He was something in that airplane," she said. "We'd be working in the field and see him coming."

I remembered back to when Mama had talked about Percy Jr.'s two children. I knew them from their occasional visits to the store and the Motocross Park East motorcycle racetrack. She said that they were 100 percent just like Percy Jr.: tall, dark-haired, good-looking boys. She went on to say that they were a lot better looking than Percy. She said that they had to take the name of another man after their mother remarried, and it made Percy mad that his grandsons had to give up the Flowers name. I asked Percy about it and he just explained that she got remarried and "them boys took a new name." Although he said it disapprovingly, he did not elaborate.

When Percy Jr. died, it was a devastating time for everyone, especially for Percy and his family.

When I was about ten years old, Mama took me to Smithfield, North Carolina, to see where Percy Jr. had been laid to rest. The tombstone was double-sided and had been made for two people. On the side where Percy Jr. lay his picture had been etched onto a smooth piece of glass. He looked young to me. I put my fingers to the picture and felt the smoothness of the glass and wondered how he could be lying there only inches from me.

I also went to visit the resting place of the Ryan several times and examined the wreckage with fascination. The first time I ever approached the plane, I watched for ghosts. I approached with caution. I'd heard about the holy ghosts in church and also about spirits, good and bad.

The old Ryan sat there upright, obviously missing the engine. It was mostly made of aluminum, which was exposed around the engine area and cockpit. The fuselage was painted black with an insignia decorating the side behind the cockpit—two flags crossed over one another. The tail was tattered and there were some bullet holes in the fuselage, probably where some hunter had taken a pot shot or two. The wings were damaged and exposed bare aluminum. The tires were knobby, flat, and looked like mud grips.

I eased up closer to the Ryan to take a better look. I cautiously approached the cockpit and looked inside. The instruments were gone, but the seat was there and was bent forward. As I peered into the cockpit area, my mind raced.

Percy Jr. actually sat right here and flew this plane. I remembered the story Mama told of him flying over the fields and what a sight it had been. *This is the plane that ended his life and caused so much pain.* I thought it strange to see the plane just sitting there in the woods. The pine trees had grown tall through the years and now completely encased the wreckage. It seemed that the Ryan had been condemned for the harm it had done and had been sentenced to sit there alone, forever hidden for its terrible deed.

Wreckage of the experimental Ryan aircraft owned by Percy Flowers Jr.

*Cockpit and seat in the
experimental Ryan*

That one dreadful day left a mother without a son and a father bereft and grieving. For better or worse, as a result of this, Percy Jr.'s two sons were whisked away from the family, and this too left a void in the Flowers lineage. These grandchildren carried the Flowers bloodline and thrived as men who built their lives as respectable members of the community with solid achievements. However, their identity might not be so easily recognized absent the name "Flowers." I knew them only as Percy's grandsons, and I always looked forward to their visits at the old store because they liked motorcycles and would take me for a spin on their bike. They were key to supporting my early interest in motorbikes.

At the time Percy told me the story, I couldn't fully understand the hurt that he felt over the loss of his son. After all, I was only eleven or twelve years old then. Since having my own two children, however, I can only imagine the pure agony he and his family must have gone through after losing Percy Jr.

Somehow his warning to me to leave airplanes alone didn't register as I later pursued a career in aviation. It was at that moment in the woods by Percy Jr.'s plane that I developed a curiosity about airplanes and flying. Perhaps it would have been better to have never seen it, to not have had an insatiable curiosity about such things. Or perhaps it was another twist in the road of life that so extraordinarily changed my course.

Percy was a man who was used to making his own decisions, and there was little discussion after he'd made up his mind. Once I had made up my mind, I, likewise, was as determined as Percy. How ironic that later in life I would become an Air Force pilot, would fly in wars, would have a fulfilling career as a commercial airline pilot, and would even play aviator roles in action movies such as *U.S. Marshals*. Flying became my passion and profession in life, but I believe Percy would not have approved. He would probably be reminded of the worst day of his life, the day his son was killed in an airplane crash, and the grief and loss that came with that horrific and senseless tragedy.

It also seemed that yet another deed in the Flowers history had shadowed Percy Flowers's true lineage. It was not enough that he suffered the loss of a son; he also had to watch as his only grandsons, at the time, went on to carry another man's name. As they grew into admirable young men, he watched and respected them quietly but never seemed to find the spirit to accept their name change. It seemed that life had a way of hiding the lineage of Percy Flowers. This was uncannily ironic and sad for a man whose life's passion had been developing noble, famous, and high-performing bloodlines in foxhounds and cocks.

Thus far in my life, my worst day was when I received the news that Percy had died. This was the end of "life as I knew it" and the beginning of a journey into the unknown. I remember thinking that I wanted to be just like Percy, and in a way, upon his death, I understood what that meant because I began to understand how he must have felt.

While Percy felt the pain of his son's death and the loss of family identity when his grandsons took a new name, I felt the pain of my father's death and the loss of family identity at not being able to bear his name. And like Percy,

I too hope to never feel pain like that again, and I pray to never lose a child.

For all of his wealth, Percy Flowers could not prevent the death of his beloved son. With the loss of Percy Jr., Percy may have asked himself "what if" questions many times. Should he have more strongly forbidden Percy Jr. to fly? Did Percy ever worry that his illegal moonshining deeds were catching up with him? Or was it, as they say, a simple twist of fate?

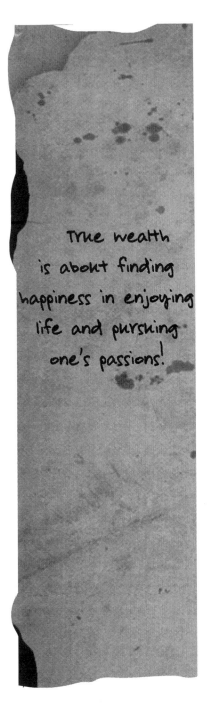

Parents usually hope that their children will do better in life than they did or be somehow better than they were—better educated, better off financially, better people! There are risks in almost every endeavor, and parents often struggle to discern how best to protect their children while also encouraging them to grow and learn and try to "be better." Parents must balance keeping children safe with making sure they also have the

opportunity for new experiences as they pursue their passions and have adventures in life. There may always be a tension between a parent's protective instincts and the passions and experiences his or her children pursue, and sometimes such questions can only be answered from the clear vision of hindsight.

Had he lived to see it, Percy would not have encouraged me to pursue my interest in aviation. But it is this passion and this pursuit of knowledge that changed my life and led to many adventures, new experiences, new friends, and a comfortable living. My life thus far has been a good one, and I have learned that being wealthy is not strictly about finances. Finding happiness and enjoying life is the wealthiest a person can be, and in that regard, I am truly a wealthy man.

I hope for you two boys to have your own adventures as you learn and go through life—and yes, I hope, as all parents do, that you "do better!"

Perry with a USAF Northrup T-38

13

THE END OF AN ERA

Dear Josh and John,

Percy had had many adversaries in his life: the law, competitors, thieves, and gamblers. None of these ever got him. But ultimately, time became the mighty moonshine king's greatest enemy. The years caught up with him and his once-strong body and piercing voice were all tamed considerably from that of a young man. His warrior spirit must have seemed jailed in an aging body as he refused to surrender to the years. His strength and character were truly as noble as that of the legend of knights. He would protect his name and his family's honor at any cost. Percy was strong in his convictions of right and wrong and refused to go the way of the newer age of gentleness and passivity. The Saturday Evening Post story of 1958 states it best: "...he was a knight born several hundred years past his time..."

He was locked in a world that had slipped away. A world that youth could only read about and wonder if such a man could have really existed at all. Time had also allowed a younger generation to come of age, and this challenged Percy's old-school ways. This newer generation was radically different from the era of hard work that he had come from. Extreme liberalism, free love and speech, government handouts, easy money and financing—all were daggers to the soul of a man who had worked and lived his entire life on principle, honor, and hard work. They came more and more each year and tried to impose their will on his land. None of these newer interlopers were successful during his reign at having their way with Percy. But Percy could not triumph over the ravages of time.

One sunny afternoon in the late 1970s I stood at the edge of the store sidewalk. Percy pulled into the store parking lot in his large Cadillac but at a much slower pace than normal. The Cadillac rolled slowly to a stop in the middle of the lot, and Percy slumped down by the steering wheel. I raced from the sidewalk to see what the problem was. I noticed the car was in neutral as it moved a little forward when I approached. I opened the door and reached in and placed the shifter into park.

"What's the matter?" I asked Percy.

He was barely able to talk and motioned with his hand for me to get his medicine from his shirt pocket. There I found a small brown medicine bottle. He was unable to reach the bottle and open it. I quickly opened it to find several unusually small pills. I took a pill out of the bottle as he just stared at me, his lower jaw shaking as he opened his mouth. He moved his jaw back and forth as it appeared he was maneuvering the pill inside his mouth. He eased back on the seat with his head leaning against the passenger door. I had never seen him like this, and I was terrified. It seemed that time was standing still, and I couldn't think what to do next.

Should I leave and run into the store to get help—or will he die while I'm gone?

By now, Reno had seen what was happening and rushed out to the car to Percy's side. I peered through the side window to see what Reno was doing.

"Can you hear me OK?" he gently asked Percy.

Several minutes went by before Percy was better and seemed to come through. We helped him sit up as he caught his balance. He slowly worked his way out of the car and managed to stand with Reno's help. Percy placed his arms over our shoulders and we helped him into the store and onto his couch.

"Will he be OK?" I asked Reno.

"Oh yeah, Dino. He OK, dis jus' a spell he has sum time," he assured me.

But Reno's reply was not so convincing. I could see that although his low, deep voice seemed solid, Reno's face was covered with deep concern. As Percy rested on the couch, I asked Reno several more times, "Will he be OK?" Percy just lay on the couch and seemed to sleep restfully.

Over the next few days, Percy appeared to be recovering. He inquired about what I wanted to do, other than make whiskey.

"Let's go to Smithfield today," he suggested. We rode there in his silver Dodge dog truck. As we crossed the Highway 70 bridge into Smithfield, he pointed to a small bar called The Brown Jug located on a street corner.

*Perry Sullivan and Percy Flowers in
1978 (behind is a gated area where
foxhounds were kept)*

*Percy behind the wheel of his silver
Dodge truck, late 1970s*

"That might make a good little place to start, Perry," he observed. I looked at the small corner building. *Whatever Percy thinks, I think.* I was still more worried about his health. I asked him about the fainting episode that had occurred in the parking lot and about the odd medicine in his pocket.

"That's just glycerin, and sometimes I have to take one," he said.

"Is it something bad?" I worried.

"No, Perry. Now you don't worry about dat," he told me.

We drove back toward the store and as we traveled through Wilson's Mills he pointed out the window.

"Now dar is good piece of land, Perry. You could have something like dat and have it made. Next week I'm getting Howard and we going to see about buying it for ya. I know the people dat own it, ole man Brown. It's rolling hills by the river and about four hundred and eighty-five acres," he said, as he continued to point.

"What will happen to me and Tammy if something happens to you, Percy?" I asked.

"Now, Perry, nothing is going to happen to me, and if it do, you and Tammy will be OK," he said. "I'm gone leave y'all da ole home place, my daddy's place and this here farm."

I couldn't talk at that point because I was so choked up at even the thought of something happening to him. So I just nodded fearfully.

Several days passed before I saw Percy at the store again.

"Perry, come on with me," he said.

We got into the truck and started toward Wilson's Mills again. We rode by the land as before and he said that he and Howard went to see ole man Brown to buy the land.

"He's selling it to me, but it's going to be in your name. They can't sign the paperwork until his wife gets back from a trip. I'm gone pay cash for it so you won't owe nothing on it," he said. "The money is in my safe. I just need to see Brown to pay him and get a deed."

Not sure what I'll do with four hundred and eighty-five acres.

"You can build a nice home on it and have a place of your own, Perry," he said, as though reading my mind. "Dar'll be enough land there for all of you to live on and you'll do just fine."

He drove down a side road to show more of the farm to me. We discussed the land on the way back to the store.

A couple of days passed and then Mama gave me the news that Percy was in the hospital, and it was not looking too good—he'd had another heart spell.

My first thoughts were, *Is he alive* and *just how serious is it?* Just the thought of Percy in the hospital defied all reason. It was hard, as they say, to wrap my mind around it. I had trouble wrestling with the idea that he could even be sick, much less die. A sort of helplessness overwhelmed me. *How could we live without him?* I regressed to primal thoughts of sheer survival. *Where will we live? Where will Curry work? Will we be kicked out of our house?* It was too early and too sudden for all of this to happen. *This can't be happening!*

I went to the store and talked with Reno, and he told me not to worry. He said that Percy would be fine. Reno and I still had mash setting in the woods that needed distilling, but how could I think of that at such a time? Reno minimized Percy's condition to protect me, I'm sure.

"We needs to run the little giant in the next couple of days, Dino," he added.

In two days, we returned to the natural spring with the little giant and ran four barrels of mash and made four cases of whiskey just as we had done before. As we ran the giant and collected the clear alcohol into buckets, we mixed the whiskey with the backings until it was perfect for sipping. Leaning over the white five-gallon bucket of whiskey that I had just made, I submerged an empty sixteen-ounce glass 7Up bottle into the bucket and watched it bubble as it filled with whiskey. Just before putting the aluminum cap on the bottle, it dawned on me that maybe I could win something on the back of the lid, so I checked. I had won nothing, but I thought it was funny and a bit odd to think about it. I placed the cap on the bottle and tightened it. Holding the bottle of whiskey up, I shook it just the way Percy and Reno had shown me. The clear whiskey bubbled from the shake. It was perfect, as it was supposed to be. I placed the small bottle of whiskey beside the other four cases and reset the mash barrels for the next run. We carried the cases to the car and carefully placed them in the boot of the car and left the woods as quietly as we could.

I kept the small 7Up bottle of whiskey with me because I knew that tomorrow I would go to visit Percy in the hospital and take it to him. When I arrived home, Mama knew what

I had been doing. The smell of whiskey told everything. It was hard to work a whiskey still all day and not smell like it. I placed the bottle of whiskey by my bed, showered, and had dinner. Mama always had something on the table to eat and always made sure we didn't go hungry.

The next morning I got up and was excited about going to visit Percy. Visiting hours were later in the morning, so there was time for breakfast. Mama was already up like always. She had eggs, bacon, and hotcakes ready and began the morning with her normal "Come on over here and eat Perry." I tried eating, but I was too nervous and my stomach was hurting a little. By 8:00 a.m., I was already in the 1981 Silver Ford Escort that Percy had bought for me and heading to the hospital with the bottle of whiskey in my coat pocket. The ride seemed to take forever, and my mind raced back and forth at what I may say to him.

I was afraid to ask about Percy's condition because I feared I would not be able to bear the real news. I couldn't imagine him in a hospital wearing hospital clothes—like other old folks that I had seen. Arriving at the hospital, I quickly found a parking spot and parked the car. Sitting there in the car, I contemplated the ramifications of being caught with the whiskey and elected to chance it, as I knew he would appreciate it. *Probably nobody would notice anyways since it was disguised,* I told myself.

Walking through a pair of electric sliding doors I looked for a receptionist desk to ask for his room number. I approached the desk and wondered what I would say if they asked if I was family. *Should I say yes or no?* After all, *yes* was the truth, and this was serious. But answering *yes* might get me into a lot of trouble if they told Percy's wife that his son had visited. I wasn't sure what to say, as I had thus far very little experience in hospitals except to know that family members were sometimes the only ones allowed to visit.

I'm seeing Percy if I have to climb up the outside wall and go through the window. Approaching the receptionist desk, I asked for Percy Flowers's room number. The receptionist told me and offered directions. I walked quickly to the elevator before she could change her mind. Walking down the hall to his room, I could see doors open and a lot of old people lying in the beds. I couldn't help looking into the open rooms and wondering what must be wrong with them. Some looked really bad and scary. Approaching his room, I noticed the door was open about a foot. I stopped for just a moment to listen for anything and then pushed the door open to enter before returning it to its partially closed position.

Percy was lying on the bed in a pair of pajamas. His shirt was pulled up slightly exposing part of his belly. The skin on his belly was whiter than his face, and his arms looked very smooth. He was wearing his glasses but did not have on his brim hat. That bothered me a little because he almost always wore his hat. As I got closer, I could see his glasses were smudged and needed cleaning.

Percy looked over and said, "Hey, Perry."

"Hey. You OK?" was all I could think of in response.

Just his presence and the thought of him there brought tears to my eyes, and I was unable to speak again for a few moments. It took all my might to keep from just bursting out crying. I'm sure he could see the hurt and terror in me. I felt like he saw right through my very soul and knew my every thought. I excused myself and found a bathroom to cry in. I prayed to God and begged him to take days from my life and give them to Percy so that we could see each other again at the store. After talking to God and crying some more, I walked over to the mirror to see that my eyes were all red. I tried to splash water onto my face and wash away the evidence of crying so that he would not notice.

Returning to the room I found Percy in the same position resting. We talked about the little giant, and I told him that we'd just run·a batch and I brought some for him to try. His eyes brightened up.

"Let's see it, Perry," he said.

I tugged at my coat pocket and pulled the 7Up bottle out, careful not to drop and break it. Slowly he reached his hand out toward me when he saw the bottle. He took it, held it up to the light from the window, and gave it a couple of shakes as he peered into the bottle. He handed it back to me.

"Open it up," he directed.

As I unscrewed the cap, the whiskey vapors quickly escaped the bottle and caught my nose by surprise. I slowly handed the bottle back to him, and he carefully placed it to his nose to smell it. Then he lowered it to his lips and tasted it.

"Perry, now this is right, this is how it suppose to taste. It *donnn't* git no better an dis," he said, pleased.

He handed the bottle back to me, and I placed it in my coat pocket. He told me not to worry, that he'd be home soon. We talked for a while, and I sat by his bedside. I couldn't help but cry some so I placed my face on the bed by his side. He placed his hand on my head as I cried and just rubbed my head. I visited for about an hour before leaving.

"Love you," I told him, just before departing.

His eyes were teared up too as he removed his glasses and wiped his eyes. He couldn't speak and just gently waved his farewell. Walking out of his room, I stood and stared at the door for a while and wondered if I would see him again.

Should I go back so that we could talk some more? I thought. *Should I question him about the seriousness of his condition?* I already knew the answers to these questions, but I wanted to hear from him. My moment of cowardliness and crying in Percy's room started to choke me, as if a man had his hands around my neck and was squeezing. Already overwhelmed, I challenged the idea of going back into his room by convincing myself that we would get a chance to talk another day.

In a few days, Percy did return home and I saw him at the store. It was good seeing him back and things seemed normal again. We talked and he told me that he and Howard had walked over ole man Brown's farm and that he was going to pay for it the next day. It seemed like just another normal day, except that it was the last day I would ever see him alive. I guess losing someone is often like that.

Percy was rushed back to the hospital the next day. That same morning, Mama answered the phone and started to cry. I knew the news couldn't be good.

She looked over at me. "He just died."

I simply couldn't believe it. It was more than I could process. I ran out to the car and hurried to the store to see Reno. People were already gathering at the news. I walked behind the store to the pond and sat under a pine tree, miserable. I realized the end of an era had arrived.

Josh and John, what I want to tell you now is something it takes many of us a lifetime to learn. You should live in the moment and love each speck of time as if it is your last. Never delay a kind word to a loved one in hopes of saying it later. Take the time to walk in the rain and stare at the clouds and enjoy each day. Always try to seek out the good as the bad is always nearby and will find you on its own. It is one of my deepest regrets that I never said some of the things I wanted to say to Percy. I never

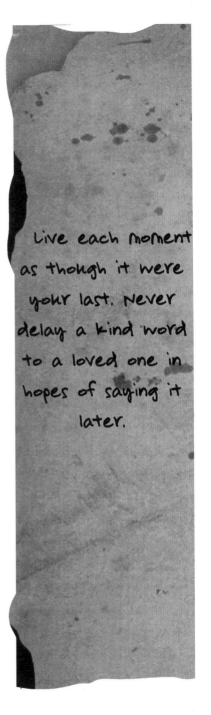

Live each moment as though it were your last. Never delay a kind word to a loved one in hopes of saying it later.

asked some of the questions I wanted to ask him. His sudden death left an emptiness in my heart that could never be filled.

*Percy Flowers standing in front
of the gated foxhound pen*

14

THE FALL

Dear Josh and John,

    While the worst day of Percy's life was the day he lost his son, the worst of day of my own life was the day I lost my father.

Percy's death in 1982 clearly marked the fall of my very existence from all security and identity. I wanted so badly to escape the mental torture of what was happening. In my mind, there was no escaping the despair, the rage of being left by him, and the constant agony of fearing the unknown. His death was more than a death. I had seen death before. This was sheer madness. I would have done anything, short of selling my soul, to avoid this time.

Until that moment in my life, there had been a place, a belonging, order, and security for me. Percy had ensured all of this. Even though we didn't carry the Flowers name, we were his by blood-right. After all, I was the "last button off of Ole Gabe's coat" as he had so often liked to say.

And it was no secret among family: it was common knowledge that Tammy and I were his children. He declared it himself. Percy's brothers and their children all knew our true identity, respected this fact, and were supportive. They were always kind to us. Even though they were of means and my sister and I were country poor, they treated us with dignity, almost with extra compassion. Still, publicly saying that my sister and I were Percy's children would have only created unnecessary humiliation for poor ole Curry, for Mama, and for Percy's wife and daughter. Curry had already carried the burden of knowing since my birth. Mama rarely referred to it and seemed embarrassed by it all. Percy's wife had worked hard at building a respectable reputation in the community and church. Furthermore, his daughter would have to suffer the public humiliation of two bastard children, a half-brother and half-sister, from her own father. It didn't matter that he had treated us as his own while he was alive, he was dead now and it was a time to cover the past. This secret was left to be forgotten and buried with Percy himself.

The morning after Percy's death, the pain of the previous day returned and I wondered if it had all been a nightmare, even though it still felt terribly real and present. I got up and went into the kitchen. Mama was sitting at the table with her face in her hands. As I entered the room she looked up, face swollen, eyes red, and just said, "What in the world are we going to do now?"

My sister was still in bed asleep. She was feeling the same agony, but hopefully she could sleep a bit longer and avoid the inevitable for a while. Curry was already up and gone to the store. That's all he knew and all he had done for thirty years. What else could he do? He had gone to his pathetic, $300-a-month job, standing at the cash register from 6:00 a.m. to 9:00 p.m. every day except Thursday for over thirty years. Imagine working in a store fourteen or fifteen hours a day, six days a week, for a man who'd fathered your children. How did he do it?

We talked that day about what we might have to do to survive. We discussed how his wife and daughter might treat us since they now controlled the farm. We realized that we were, to them, simply constant reminders of Percy's infidelity that had caused their own suffering and humiliation throughout the years on the farm. Would they make us leave or would they sell the store? Would Curry still make his measly $300 per month? What would happen?

Percy Flowers's death was the highlight of the news media throughout the entire area. The mighty man who had built a robust moonshining empire was now laid to rest. All of the community spoke well of him and of his good deeds to the needy and his community. His funeral and final farewell was to be held in Clayton. I asked Mama if we could go and she replied in tears, "Of course we gonna go." I thought about his wife and daughter and how they might treat us at the funeral.

On the day of the funeral, we dressed our very best just as if we were going to church. We all climbed into Curry's green Ford truck and headed toward the funeral home. As we arrived, I thought about seeing his wife and daughter and how difficult that would be but not so much that it could prevent me from saying my final goodbyes to Percy. The funeral home was full of folks, some of whom I didn't recognize. Entering the funeral home, I noticed the coffin to the right. The lid was open, but his face was not visible from where I stood. The terror left me for a moment, and I stood in a crowd of people who I felt didn't have half the right to be there that I did. But I did not bear the Flowers name and so I went unnoticed to outsiders.

No one would offer condolences to me for my loss. True loneliness began to set in as I stood among the crowd. Percy was my father, and I loved him as much as a child could. My mind raced as I considered how to approach the coffin and say goodbye without others watching that last precious moment. I had a notion to simply talk to him and hope that his lifeless body could somehow hear me. I had always feared ghosts and things like that, but this was different.

I approached the coffin slowly as people stood around it and talked. Percy's face began to come into my view and then his chest and hands. His suit was pressed firmly and lay neatly on his still body. He reminded me of the portrait that hung in his home. I had seen it a few times as a child when Percy and I visited to get things. There was neither smile nor frown—his expression was just neutral. His lips looked redder than normal and there was a faint appearance of makeup. At the top left of his forehead was a black dot that I couldn't remember being there. Beside it was a red dot that I remembered always being there. For some odd reason, this small detail was the proof that I somehow needed to distinguish this from a nightmare so that I knew it was really him. As I stood before him, my throat felt completely blocked, and I couldn't have spoken had my life depended on it. It felt that all eyes were watching, so I looked left and right to see if there was a moment to touch his hand without being noticed. Reaching down, somehow, I overcame the fear that he was dead and I placed my hand over the top of his hands. They were cool but not cold as I expected them to be. They felt stiff and not warm the way I remembered them feeling when he held me as a child.

Looking down at him I prayed.

Please just open your eyes or move a little and let me know that you can see me and understand so I won't be alone. I promise I won't be afraid if you do. I won't even say anything. Just let me know that you are here.

A tear ran out of my right eye and dropped onto his sleeve. I wondered how long could I stand there. I felt rushed to leave but couldn't. I would never see him again, and I didn't think that my feet would move me even if I willed them to do so. How long had I been standing there? Just another minute would be OK. As I forced my body to move away from the coffin, I stood nearby and stared back for a while. I silently talked with God and asked if I could go with him and not stay there. Was there some magical or heavenly way, I asked God, that I could be allowed to go with Percy? I also asked God to tell Percy that I missed him, just in case he couldn't see me here. From that moment, I can only remember a long line of cars to the burial site. I can't even remember the gravesite now nor any words anyone said at the burial. But the memory of him in the coffin will always be with me as strong as the memories of him as a father.

Several days passed, and I returned to the store. The local sheriff, Cobb, came by while I was there. He walked slowly on the sidewalk, but his jaws still shook from his steps as they always did. He called me and Reno aside to talk. He removed the cigar he was chewing and told us that we needed to leave the whiskey alone now that Percy was dead. He warned us that if we got caught by the feds that there was nothing he could do for us. As he talked, I noticed that his lips were still discolored with spots and that his teeth were stained, probably from the cigars just as they had been years ago when I was just a boy. Sheriff Cobb had known me ever since I was born and he also knew the secret. When Sheriff Cobb left, I asked Reno about the little giant and the barrels of mash still in the woods.

"Noooo, Dino. Better jus' leave it there," he said.

No need to question Reno—my mind was already made

up. That was my whiskey still, given to me by Percy, and I wasn't leaving it in the woods. The next day, early, I got up and removed all the seats out of my Ford Escort except the driver's seat. I collected a pipe wrench, a monkey wrench, screwdrivers, and four cases of empty jars. The morning was cold, but I knew the mash was ready to be run. I loaded the tools and the empty jars into the back of the car and placed a sheet over them as I headed toward the little giant. Regardless of the risks, I was determined to collect the still. Getting caught was a chance I would have to take.

I eased the little Escort down the dirt path and looked for fresh tracks on the dirt and anything out of the ordinary. Approaching the side path, I backed the car under some limbs and turned the ignition off just as Reno had always done. Opening the door outside sounded quieter than it ever had before. Careful not to slam the door, I gently pushed it closed and latched it with my body weight and moved to the back. I opened the trunk and began carrying the cases and tools into the woods by the whiskey still. As always, I moved slowly and listened for any sounds. Occasionally the sound of a car from Buffalo Road echoed through the woods. The still seemed untouched and there was plenty of propane in the tanks to fire the burner and do the job. It was time to work. I removed the boiler cap and checked the water level in the boiler. It needed some, so I filled it with five-gallon buckets, making several trips to the spring.

As soon as the boiler was full, I lit the burner to start heating the water while I filled the cooker with mash. The burner was slightly rusty where it had set since the last run. As the burner lit off, the woods came alive with the roar of burner exhaust. The tree limbs overhead began to sway, but I didn't worry about catching them on fire from the burner exhaust since the leaves had already fallen off. I moved quickly as I knew it would take all day to run the mash and remove the still. The head of the cooker came off easily, and I filled it with mash, carrying two five-gallon buckets of mash at a time. It only took about five trips to fill the cooker. The fresh mash smelled good going into the cooker, and I thought of Percy for a moment.

As the water was heating, I filled the worm barrel to the top, hoping that it would take a little extra time to get hot since keeping the worm barrel full of cold water was the hardest part of running the giant. I also set two extra five-gallon buckets of water by the barrel so it would be ready to pour in. In just a few minutes the little giant began to burble and rumble a little and it was almost time. I checked to ensure that the main line valve was open to prevent an explosion and then waited at the worm outlet for the first few drops to come out.

Soon the whiskey began to flow into the catch bucket. In just a few more minutes steam began to swirl around the top of the worm barrel as the worm began to warm up. I adjusted the gas tank valve to lower the burner flame but still have enough fire to run the whiskey. This gave me enough time to keep the worm barrel water changed out so as not to lose any whiskey through steam.

For the next hour I worked hard at emptying and filling the worm barrel, adjusting the burner and monitoring the whiskey flow. As soon as the backings ran, I quickly put the blowout hose in the fifty-gallon wooden mash barrel, opened the blowout valve, and closed the main line valve. The large blowout hose again wrestled me like an anaconda, but I held it into the barrel until nothing came out except steam and a few strong puffs. This time the mash barrels would not be sweetened again. It took four runs to distill all the mash into whiskey.

I never before realized how much easier it was with Reno there. After the last run, I turned the burner off and mixed the whiskey until it was perfect for sipping. The still needed time to cool down, so I carried the whiskey cases to the car and loaded them. I drove the cases to my house and hid them in the woods and returned to the giant. It was still warm as I began to disassemble it into pieces. At that point, making drag marks in the woods wasn't a concern since the giant had run its last batch there. I dragged each piece through the woods to where the car sat. The boiler and the cooker weighed well over a hundred pounds each and the gas tanks were all heavy steel. Piece by piece, I dragged them to the car. It took six trips to move the little giant home in my stripped-out Escort. I was covered with the smell of whiskey and dirty from all the work.

As I pulled onto Buffalo Road and began to drive toward Highway 42, a highway patrol car pulled up behind me. I felt myself begin to sweat and I could hear my own heartbeat as I glanced into the rear mirror to see if he turned his lights on to stop me. He followed me all the way to Highway 42, about three miles. As I turned left toward Clayton, he continued straight toward the small community of Archer

Lodge. Never before in my life had I felt so relieved. The day was over, and the little giant rested in the barn behind my house.

Over the next few days I had Reno sell the whiskey and tried to put the thought of making whiskey behind me. It wasn't profitable for all the work involved, and the risks were high, as mentioned by Sheriff Cobb. But even though it was risky and the work was hard, we needed the money.

I moved the still to Clayton and set up underground beneath a tobacco barn. I knew a man there that enjoyed the taste of corn whiskey. He allowed me to use the underground pit beneath his barn. To get down into the pit, there was a small trap opening in the wooden floor. It was just large enough to get the boiler and cooker through. I carried the whiskey still there piece by piece and lowered it through the small opening into the underground pit. There was just enough room to set up the still and four fifty-gallon barrels. I had a single light in the ceiling powered from the old man's house, and I used a long water hose to get the water to the barn when I needed it.

There was no ventilation or windows in the pit, just the small trap-door opening. When I fired the little giant up the first time, it nearly started a fire from the boiler exhaust blast. I had to build an exhaust deflector from an old tobacco pack-house burner flue. The heat was unbearable when the burner was running. Changing the worm barrel water was a full-time job and then some. I had to take quick breaks and climb through the trap door opening to sit and cool from the burner heat. Working the still underground was nearly unbearable as the heat from the boiler was fierce and the ground was always wet from water. It was like a constant sauna bath for several hours at a time. For several months I kept the still running to keep money coming in as I looked for a regular job. Of course I paid the old man with whiskey for the use of his barn and pit.

I finally fully realized the lesson Percy wanted to teach me. Running a whiskey still was damn hard and not something I wanted to do forever. Too bad I learned all this a little too late. Curry continued working at the store as Percy's wife and daughter began to liquidate his assets. The prized foxhounds and fighting cocks were sold at a large auction. A lifetime collection gone in a few days. But who needed fox hounds and fighting cocks now? They were just extra mouths to feed. And even though it is said that Percy made millions I'm sure it all was exaggerated. When he died he was land rich and money poor.

Within a few months, Curry brought home the news that the store was being rented out and that he would soon no longer have a job. Did all of Curry's years there mean so little? Was there no dignity or humanity? The man had given most of his life there with no retirement or benefits— and now this! It seemed more than a business transaction; it seemed an invitation to leave. His services were no longer needed.

There was no way we could live there any longer. We weren't even sure how we would feed ourselves. But Curry kept quiet as he always had. It was a quality he'd learned early on. Now, at sixty-five years old, he got a job with Charles Lewis Barns in Rock Ridge, cutting grass and doing odd jobs around a tractor garage. Charles owned a tractor company and campground. He also enjoyed fox-hounds and knew that Curry, from his years of experience with Percy, knew a lot about hunting.

We moved into a small cinder block house by Rock Ridge. Shortly after Percy's death and with no prospects, my sister Tammy joined the navy. Perhaps she felt she would escape the pain of losing Percy as well as the shame of being unacknowledged as his daughter and therefore unable to grieve openly. I got a job in a factory building carburetors on an assembly line. The trip to work was fifty-eight miles, and I would leave at 3:15 a.m. to be at work by 5:00 a.m. The days were long, and I'd get home around 7:00 p.m. after a twelve-hour shift. Within a year, I started working with a construction crew laying water and sewer line. I had to work so we could pay the bills and eat. It was a difficult two years without Percy, and life was changing forever as I distanced myself from the only home I'd ever known.

15

RECOVERY

Dear Josh and John,

It would take a long time to recover from Percy's death. There was much more to it than simply mourning the death of a parent. The psychological scars from illegitimacy and its accompanying isolation are forever present. Also, I was beginning to realize that my own personal neglect for, and lack of interest in, a serious education left me at a real disadvantage for attending college. I could barely read, write, and comprehend at a sixth- or seventh-grade level. I had not taken my public schooling seriously, as it was of little interest to me at the time. Although the years in competition racing broadened my outlook, they had done little to prepare me for a formal education.

Percy, before his death, had urged me to attend North Carolina State University to become a veterinarian. He offered to pay for the education and set me up in business on the farm. I wasn't ready for that and knew it. His untimely death kept him from securing the Brown's farm, so my family had no place to call home. At the time, it seemed all hope was gone. Working a factory job was a far cry from being a veterinarian.

The question for me at this crossroads in my life was this: Now that Percy was dead, and we had no financial— or community—support, what could I do to recover from my desperate situation? What should I do? It has been said that desperate times require desperate measures. This was especially true for me at this point in my life.

Mama's persistent words, "All you need is God and a good education," rang out louder than ever. Although I was not sure what to do, it was clear that a job was necessary and it needed to be one not so far from home. My expenses were few as I lived temporarily with Mama and Curry. For the first time ever, Curry showed some support. He called a relative and helped me get a job laying water and sewer lines. Working in a trench behind a backhoe was hard work, but it was near home. The money wasn't as good as it was making whiskey, but at least I didn't have to be continually looking over my shoulder, worrying about breaking the law.

On one unusually hot day, I walked behind the backhoe, my shirt wet with sweat. As I bent over to join the water line behind the backhoe, sweat ran into my eye. As I stood up to wipe it clear, I noticed how bright and beautiful the sky appeared.

Up high in the sky I saw a perfect white line—a contrail from a jet streaking across the sky. This was a moment of clarity, beauty, and hope. That moment changed the course of my life just as clearly as Percy's life was changed that moonlit night when he met Lester at the whiskey still. As Percy's words came echoing back about leaving those airplanes alone, I knew what to do next.

My mind was made up. *I'm quitting this backbreaking, pipe-laying job to get an education and learn to fly!*

After a visit to the local airport, I understood immediately that it took a great deal of money to learn to fly. This would have to be a slow process. I found a job at the Pepsi-Cola plant in Raleigh. The money wasn't great, but at least

I wasn't working in a trench behind a backhoe. Over the next year, my earnings and time were dedicated toward flying lessons at the Johnston County airport. Under the supervision of Mr. Arthur West, a retired WWII pilot, I learned the basics of flying. Mr. West recommended military flying. This sounded good to me—fly fast airplanes and let the government pay for it! Within a few months, I earned a private license in a Cessna 152 and later an instrument rating in his Mooney M20C. Flying was fun and offered a welcome outlet to all the numbness of the past couple of years. Although flying came naturally, the education and knowledge that would be required to succeed presented me with some obstacles.

I looked into entering the navy or army as a pilot, but these all required a four-year college degree. Up until this point, I had not thought about the need for an education to enter the military. People around home said the military was for people who couldn't do anything else and for those with only the choice of going to jail or serving. All I knew about the military was that a few people on the farm limped around from war wounds. They were all army grunts, ground-pounders, or riflemen who had served in World War II, Korea, or Vietnam.

Mama had always said, "You need to go to college, Perry, or you just going to work around all your life." My sister had already joined the navy and had some experience there. She warned me to go to college before joining the service or I would have very little chance of actually flying airplanes. That was all that I knew about the military. Living in the country, we simply didn't have access to the knowledge for making such decisions. People around the farm didn't know much about things outside of farming and hard work. I had the basics of flight instruction and decided to get a four-year degree so that I could join the military to fly. So I attended community college and later got accepted to East Carolina University.

Before I left for the university, Mama told me, "We ain't got nothing to give you, but I know you can do it if you really want to."

With that piece of advice, I quit my Pepsi job, packed up my clothes, and moved into a dorm room at East Carolina University on the hill. I got a job at a local bar as a cook and dish washer. I could eat there and take it out of my pay each week. After deductions, I ended with about twenty-five dollars a week. My original attraction to East Carolina University was that it offered Air Force Reserve Officer Training Corp, or ROTC. I joined the Air Force ROTC and learned to march and drill. As opposed to some of my classmates who had time to enjoy college, I worked and took extra classes to finish college in just three and a half years. Because of my lack of early education and poor rural upbringing, I was virtually illiterate and this made university coursework especially challenging. There was little time for parties or hanging out with friends.

Lieutenant Colonel Paul Knoke was the professor of aerospace studies and the one responsible for my recruitment. He had been an English professor at the Air Force Academy. He seemed amused by my Southern drawl and my terrible lack of reading and writing skills. These must have presented a real challenge for him. There was a chance I could become an Air Force pilot if I performed well enough on the Air Force Officer Qualifying Test. The test was difficult, but I passed and received a pilot slot to attend pilot training upon finishing college.

Lieutenant Colonel Knoke supported and guided me over the next three years. He understood that determination was within me. He said that he could teach me to read and write well enough to become a pilot. After all, he said, he had never met many pilots who could read or spell very well anyway! I really knew very little about the military but all of this sounded interesting.

College was exciting, and the goal of attending pilot training made it worthwhile. During my second year in college, I met and married a young woman from Maryland. She was from a middle-class family, and we worked together to finish college and start our lives. She was smart, and, to my great amazement, she somehow found me interesting enough to marry. She was different in every way from the people I knew around the farm. Her ways were kind, and she didn't understand the prejudices of the South. She knew my background and submitted to the formidable challenge of correcting my bad habits and refining my wild character.

I finished college in three and a half years and was commissioned as a second lieutenant by the US Air Force. Mama had her prayer answered: I got an education. Even Curry attended my commencement ceremony. Times were changing. I secured a pilot training slot at Reese Air Force base in Lubbock, Texas, and we moved to Texas to start military flight training.

My previous private flying instruction helped tremendously in the early stages of air force flight training. Lieutenant Terry Smith, T-37 instructor pilot, had the initial challenge of turning a country boy into a jet pilot. Terry enjoyed motorcycles, and we connected right away. He was a hard-ass, a yeller, and a helmet slapper. He knew just how, with a single look, to make a person feel one inch tall. His father had been a colonel in the air force when Terry was a boy, so he was no stranger to the military. Terry was exactly what I needed to get through military pilot training. He could never break me, but he sure could "put fear" into me. He had a gift for insulting people down to complete humility but still maintaining their respect. Oddly enough, Terry demonstrated complete confidence in my skills even when I didn't. As he taught me to fly the air force basic trainer, the T-37 in a fast-paced learning environment, he was remarkably patient and demonstrated superb instructor skills.

This was a very challenging year, but my reward was to graduate and become an air force pilot. The air force was all about teamwork, patience, leadership, respect, and doing your very best. Doing my best was about the only attribute that I had, along with a great deal of determination. Over the years I observed, studied, and learned to become an officer and a respectable citizen according to military standards. This was no small endeavor and took a great deal of time.

After pilot training, the air force sent me to fly KC-10 Extenders at Seymour Johnson Air Force Base in Goldsboro, North Carolina, just a few miles from the farm where I had grown up. The KC-10 was the newest and most sought-after air refueler in the air force inventory. In 1989, I finished KC-10 aircraft training and began flying this monster plane as my first major weapons system in the 911th Air Refueling Squadron. Shortly after entering the squadron, the Iraqi war began.

I kissed my lovely wife goodbye and headed for the Middle East. As the war kicked off, the possibility of death or becoming a prisoner of war seemed for the first time very real and very much an eye-opener. Over the next few years, I flew the KC-10 during the war and for war support.

As I steadily progressed through the ranks and command positions, the military became a way of life. I flew all over the globe and often returned to the Middle East to support the ongoing war effort there.

On one particular mission, the number two engine shelled out. We finessed the crippled KC-10 over Middle Eastern borders into Saudi Arabia, where we spent several glorious days in the same flight suits as we waited for a new engine.

Throughout several tours there, I learned to dislike chicken and rice. I believe I ate enough chicken and rice to last a lifetime. One thing the service does is feed their people well. Chicken and rice just happened to be what all too often was served.

Perry Sullivan in the cockpit of the MD-80

In 1994, we moved to New Jersey, and I flew the KC-10 at McGuire AFB. By 1997, I exited active duty and joined the air force reserves and continued to fly the tanker and later the C-9 in medical and congressional support. The military offered opportunities that I could never have dreamed of. Military people are the most honorable people that I will ever have the privilege of knowing. They are committed to a better way of life for all, even if it means giving up their own lives in the process. In the military mindset, doing what is right is always the course of action you should take, even if it means great personal sacrifice.

In 1998, my wife and I moved to the Midwest, and our first son, Josh Perry, was born. In 2001, a second son was born, John Percy. Both were named after their grandfather, Percy.

In 2000, I was hired as a pilot by a major commercial airline. It seemed the years on the farm were so long and so far behind me, yet I often thought about those times as somehow incomplete or unfinished. Their memories were always on my mind. There was never any closure and there never would be—only an abrupt and sorrowful exit from the only life I had ever known.

Twenty-five years had passed and I was now a young man. I've heard stories and seen glimpses of the land ruled by the mighty moonshine king Joshua Percy Flowers. I could never forget the place I had always called home. From time to time I would visit Mama who moved to a nearby town, or chat with Tammy while she served in the navy. As time passed, Reno and I grew apart as our lives took different paths.

As a father with children of my own, I began to feel the gnawing need to resolve unfinished business and to set the record straight about my heritage and that of my sons. Knowing the past and still hiding my secret, I decided I had to revisit the farm.

16

FACING THE TRUTH

Dear Josh and John,

Vacation arrived and you two were just five and seven years old. You wanted to visit the Atlantic Ocean and play on the beach. The journey would take us by the old farm on Highway 42 East, en route to Atlantic Beach. We planned the trip, and your mother and I discussed stopping by the farm and showing you where I had grown up. Despite tensions about the past related to the secret I harbored, this seemed to make sense.

Would this be the time to reveal my true identity? To face the uncomfortable ghosts of the past? Although it has

253

been said that where one grew up always feels like home, I felt uneasy but still resolute that this was the right thing to do.

"Did you remember your Gameboys?" I asked after loading the car. It was a long ride to Carolina.

"Yea, Dad, we have them," they replied in unison.

We were excited and a little nervous.

"Did we lock the door?" Joanie and I questioned one another. Would the kid up the street remember to feed the guinea pigs?

The hours ticked by as we enjoyed the ride through the Tennessee and Carolina mountains. We spent the night on the Blue Ridge Parkway and woke up to a foggy morning. We reloaded the car and were soon on the road again.

"Hey look, a Cracker Barrel. Ready for breakfast?" We enjoyed breakfast and discussed the day ahead.

"Honey, do you think it will be OK to ride around the farm and have a look?" Joanie asked me.

"Well, I think so," I told her. It had been a long time and there was a lot of change. When I'd last visited Reno many years before, I drove around and some of the roads no longer even existed.

We chatted about the visit, and I realized that I was a bit fearful of visiting the place I had once called home. Not only was I anxious over the possible changes to the landscape, I also was anxious about facing my past and the unfinished business of somehow accepting who I was and confronting the true identity I'd left there so many years ago. This was the land my father worked so hard for. The land he had made a place for so many folks to live and work upon. It seemed odd that now I would be just another stranger passing through—a stranger to all but a few folks who knew my secret.

By now, Percy's heir had developed the land into a progressive town with hundreds of homes and a modern, middle-class community. She was the owner now and Percy was no more. I would be nothing more than the opening of an old wound. I remembered Reno's comments from my last visit about how my biological half sister felt about my sister Tammy and me.

"She don't like you and Tammy and don't want you around here," he had told me.

Yes, I was a bit fearful of the unknown but felt deserving of a visit. My half sister knew the secret, and I wondered how she would react to me returning, even for a brief time. Would she be kind or not? Would this be stirring up a hornet's nest? Reno had once warned me to "let a dead cat in the road just lay there and not mess with it." I felt so cheated at how Percy's death had left us damaged and heartbroken, not just financially but emotionally and even existentially. We were simply wiped away in a moment, never to be considered again.

After a long ride, we traveled east on Highway 42, the same road I'd traveled so many times with Percy. As we passed the location where the motocross track once had been, I noticed a large home with security gates guarding the entrance. There was no recognizable part of the track or track entrance left. A little further down, we crossed the Neuse River Bridge, about at the spot where the highway patrol had stopped me on my minibike so many years before. The field where I'd hunted as a boy was now a school surrounded with streets.

We slowed down, and I could not find the old dirt-road entry to our home place on Motorcycle Road. We continued east on 42 for several miles, noticing that home developments had consumed the roadside. All of these places had been open fields and forest at one time.

I turned our car left onto a road that also used to lead to our home. At last there was some relief from the unsettledness of all the change. The road looked much the same but had been paved over. Percy had allowed me to drive his truck so many times on this road. When Percy drove it, we raced around the corners and down the straights as I leaned out the window and watched the billowing dust trail follow us, knowing it would consume us the moment we stopped. I looked into the mirror, but there was no dust trail.

More new housing developments sprawled across the hills.

"Hey, look, there are the barns where we used to cure tobacco!" I said.

The barns had been transformed into single-unit houses. We approached the old home site where I had grown up. As we pulled over and off the road, I could barely make out the tattered asphalt driveway. The house was gone and only slightly visible sections of the driveway remained. One old oak tree stood beside where the house had once been. My grandfather used to sit under those trees every Sunday after church when he visited. The barns were all gone. A large, grass-covered mound of dirt sat behind where the house had been. It looked like the house and barns had been torn down and everything buried, as if someone had wanted to remove a blemish from the modern community and perhaps from the past as well. Behind the home site was another large oak tree.

I shut off the car and we all got out. The car interior chime went off because I had left the keys in the car. It seemed odd—as if the shrill sound was out of place. I was standing there, yet was also catapulted back thirty years, and the modern car key chime just didn't belong. We walked toward the middle of the lot, and I considered the possibility that we may be trespassing. *What a peculiar feeling, me, trespassing on the property that I grew up on.* I couldn't stop walking as I spotted the large oak tree still standing behind our house's site.

"Right here, right here, this is the exact spot where Percy unloaded the motorbike after we returned from Honda of Raleigh," I explained to the boys. *This is where we stood under the shade of the large oaks as he chewed his White Owl cigar, told me that the motorcycle could hurt me, and smiled at my delight.*

I looked upon the ground where we'd once stood as if I might see something that we'd left there so long ago. All the chicken houses were gone. My sons were running and playing foolishly over the same area where I had played as a child. The thought of trespassing crossed my mind again. I quickly shut out the thought and quietly recalled all the contented times we'd spent here as a family. There was little physical evidence of the past, even though the events were clearly recurring in my memory as I stood there. As I slowly walked back to the car I saw the remains of the driveway where I had once sat and carved my name into the asphalt with a hammer and nail. So many times Percy had sat in his truck right there, on that spot, and we'd talked.

Being at this strange juncture in physical time and mental space was emotionally overwhelming. I closed my eyes and tried to imagine exactly what Percy's voice had sounded like and how he'd smelled as he rubbed his cheek against mine. At that moment, I could still hear him and feel him just like it was yesterday. If only I opened my eyes and he could be here for just a few minutes to explain.

I was jolted back to reality when I noticed two people walking down the sidewalk along the road's edge, and again, I considered whether we should be there. We got into the car and slowly drove away. Watching the roadside, vivid memories of the landscape came to mind and I found it difficult to adjust to all the change at once.

We continued toward the store and turned onto Buffalo Road by Percy's old home place. I couldn't believe my eyes. The old cedar tree was still there. It had always reminded me of a large wolf. Percy told me that he and his wife had planted that tree there when they were first married.

The "lone wolf" cedar tree had remained standing all those years. Just past the tree was the site where our first home had stood, down the dirt path from Buffalo Road. This was where I had been born and where Percy visited so many times. This was where he'd gooched me and rubbed his bearded face against my cheeks that Christmas in 1967 after I gave him the bottle of Hai Karate. It was where he first asked me if I knew that I was "the last button off Ole Gabe's coat" and where he introduced me to my half sister after he gave me her picture from the ashtray of the big Cadillac. This was where my story all began in 1961, as my mother and he embraced and plotted their affair. Could they have possibly considered the long-lasting effects their coupling and secret would have on so many lives?

We turned around and headed back toward the store. Just out in those woods was where I'd visited my first whiskey still with Reno. It was a large operation capable of running several thousand gallons of mash at a time and served as my first look at a large whiskey still in operation. Now houses sat on the once-sacred ground.

We traveled back to the store, which had been completely rebuilt after Percy's death. It was now a store and offices. Just like her father, Percy's daughter ran the operation from the same spot. There was even a liquor store on the premises. We parked and walked into the store. I felt overwhelmed just by standing on the same ground that I had considered my own so many years before. I could still imagine Percy sitting in his big chair when all the men watched or listened to the baseball games and NASCAR races. This was the same place where Reno timed me as I raced around the store counters for a record time. I looked across the store parking lot and remembered Percy slumped over in the big Cadillac—right there in the parking lot.

Looking across Highway 42, Percy's home looked practically unchanged. I remembered that one winter he slipped on the ice-covered sidewalk leading down to the store. I could see it all clearly in my mind uncluttered by the current change. It was challenging to take it all in.

How I would have loved to have had just another moment with Percy!

We walked down the sidewalk to the legal whiskey store and went in. A woman stood behind the counter. By the corner, to my surprise, sat Reno. He looked so old, but I recognized him immediately. He looked up and recognized me.

"Good gracious to life I want you to see dis," he said.

In his deep voice he sounded just like he always had.

"How you doing, Dino, my boy?"

I could barely respond. My childhood friend was right before me.

"Who is these fine-looking boys with you today?" Dino had never met my sons.

"This is Josh Perry, he's seven, and this is John Percy, he's five," I replied.

"Dino, can you believe it? Weez selling whiskey here legally. Mr. Percy wouldn't know what to thank if he was here today." He laughed.

"Reno, I never thought I would see legal whiskey being sold here. It sure has changed around here."

"Shaw has, my boy, shaw has."

"I sure miss Percy. I'd like to spend a few minutes with him just one more time," I said wistfully.

"I'd like to spend a whole lot of days with him, dat's right. What you think he say now, Dino?" Reno said.

"Don't know, Reno, but I'd sure like to see."

Josh and John had started playing in the store and being silly, as John got a little mad with his brother. John's quick temper flared up and he was ready to take on his older brother. Reno simply smiled. We talked for a few minutes about old times and all the change.

Reno looked closely at John Percy. "Now, Dino, that little rascal is just like Mr. Percy. He already gots his ways."

Dino, you're right about that, and why shouldn't he be just like his grandfather? After all, he was Percy's blood. As I talked with Reno, I realized the tragedy of it all.

Before leaving, I said to him, "This was all so unfair to be left like this."

Reno knew exactly what I meant. I was referring to the victims of the affair and how Tammy and I had been left alone as children, shunned after Percy's death. I also asked Reno if he would be willing to talk privately at some point.

"Dino, nothing I'd like better," he said.

We left the store that day to finish our vacation and then return to the Midwest.

Later I planned a trip to visit with Reno myself—a trip that would reveal some surprising facts about the past and clear up some questions. On December 30, 2006, I called my lifelong friend, Scotty Flowers, who still lived in the area near the store. I asked him if he could arrange to bring Reno to his home as I needed a place to speak privately with him.

Scotty was quick to oblige. I knew that it would be difficult to get some free time with Reno at the store where he spent most of his day. Tammy had already been warned by Reno that Percy's daughter, now the real estate millionaire of that area, had said that Tammy was not welcome on the farm. I wondered if that applied to me as well. After all, I had spoken with her once or twice since our father's death, and she had been pleasant. Her kindness during those talks was welcome and had been a relief. However, stirring up the past might demand some difficult reconciliation.

Other than my mother, Reno was the only one left who held the knowledge to my questions. I had high respect for my old friend Reno and did not want to cause him any trouble that might result from our visit. Reno still lived at Percy's old home place and worked around on the farm for Percy's daughter. His life and all that he had ever been revolved around that farm and I did not want to endanger that. The days of brutal racism and open hatred had all but vanished. Reno had stood the test of time and all the new folks knew and respected him as "Howard," the man who made whiskey for Percy. Reno lived there now and basically manned the king's throne. He was the last volume of knowledge for an era that was all but gone. In the back of my mind I knew that we would be digging up old skeletons that had been buried and mostly forgotten for many years by all but a few souls.

Scotty called me and told me that Reno had said, "Get down here right away." Within two hours of that phone call, I was in my car and heading back to the farm to meet with Reno. As the hours crept by on the road to North Carolina, I thought of all the times I'd had there on the farm. My mind raced forward even though my car was limited to the posted highway speeds. I couldn't get there fast enough.

I knew that Reno's death would forever seal his lips of the knowledge I needed. Had I waited too long? The hours passed slowly as I ticked off the exits on Highway 40. I wondered why it had taken so long to build up the courage to talk to Reno. After driving fourteen hours, I entered Clayton, North Carolina, around five a.m. on December 31 and decided to go straight to Mama's place in Smithfield, just another fifteen-minute drive. Arriving at her modest, government low-income apartment, I approached the aluminum screen door and knocked on it several times. There was no immediate answer, so I stepped off the sidewalk, squeaked past the shrubbery and tapped on her bedroom window. It was still quiet outside. The air was still and the morning traffic had not yet begun to bustle and flow.

After another minute, the door cracked open slowly and she sleepily peered out. Once she saw it was her son, she moved as swiftly as a young schoolgirl. Her smile was large and her eyes tearful as she told me how glad she was to see me. Mama immediately hugged me, and just as she'd always done when I was a little boy, she wanted to fix breakfast right away. I asked her to let me sleep for just a few hours and then we would have breakfast. By mid-morning, Mama woke me, asking if I was going to sleep all day. I didn't want to waste the day, even though I was still very sleepy from driving all the night.

Mama hadn't changed. She bombarded me with questions as soon as I woke up.

"You want some coffee, baby, or hotcakes? I can make you hotcakes in a minute!"

"No, Mom, just let me wake up for a minute first please."

She continued to ask if I wanted anything to eat or drink and asked about my wife and children. She was so excited she couldn't sit still.

When I suggested we go out for lunch, she thought for a moment and then acted as if I had insulted her cooking.

"Well, Perry, I have some collards in the 'frigerator and I can cook us some chicken and make you some of yer favorite cornbread," she told me. "You know you ain't going to get food as good as I can cook."

I agreed with her but told her that she deserved to go out for a change. She seemed pleased with this, and we talked for a while longer before going. Of course, she wanted to know how her grandchildren and my family were doing. I explained in some detail that everyone was doing fine. She explained how much she missed the grandchildren, and I asked her if she would like to travel out to visit for a while.

"I just ain't able to go out there to visit," she said, referring to a long-promised trip to the Midwest. "But I'm glad you came here."

I explained that the purpose of my visit was to talk to Reno about Percy and that I had some questions I wanted to ask her also. I told her the questions would be about Percy and requested her permission to ask anything.

"Now, Perry, you ought to leave all that ole mess alone and let bygones be bygones," she advised.

"Well, Mom, I want to know something. How could you have me and Tammy with Percy while you were married to Curry?"

She looked directly at me and took on a serious expression. She pointed her finger in the air and finally spoke. "Now, Perry, I wahn't even havin' sex with Curry. He slept in a different bed for several years before you and Tammy were ever even born. And, you know I w'ant no whore or runaround. I just wanted, like any married woman, to have me some young'uns. Me and Percy tried for a while to have you two children."

I was stunned. It was a shock to hear Mama say "sex," and I was just as shocked at her candidness. I thought back and couldn't remember a time that just the two of us had talked without people around. I decided to press forward.

"What did Curry say about you being pregnant and you weren't even having sex with him?" I asked, as gently as I could.

"I don't know. He never even said one bad word to me, ever, about it, but he never even went to the hospital when you were born."

Again, I was stunned. "How could he not say anything? He was no fool and had to know that you were having an affair."

"I told him that I wanted some children and I was glad that I was having one. God knows how much I wanted children," she said. "I prayed to God to forgive me for treating Curry like I did, 'cause I know it hurt him, but he never said a bad word to me. I guess he knew how much I wanted some young'uns and him and me could never have none. You two children was all I had to live for and you two was my life."

"What about Percy?" I asked.

She glanced slightly away and thought for a moment. "Well, we all knew him when we were little and he started out just as poor as the rest of us, but he was a good-hearted man. He knew I wanted children, and he wanted, you, too.

"Percy loved you and Tammy," she went on. "One time he came over and wanted to take you with him. He kept you all day, and when he brought you home, you were missing your shoe. I asked him what in the world he did with you all day and he said that he just wanted to show you off to some of his friends. He was proud of you because his first boy was 'gone on' from a plane crash, and that like to killed him. So, you should know that he was so happy to have you, Perry, and we had to go through a lot havin' you and Tammy. Nobody will ever know the heartache we went through."

It was good to see Mama and talk with her. We talked about other things and then went for lunch to a local restaurant. We talked more at length as we ate and reminisced about old times. Mama never had changed. Talking with her was like stepping back in time. Her words are always simple, straightforward, and earnest.

We drove back to her apartment after lunch. I loaded my suitcase into the car and we said goodbye. As always, she stood on the sidewalk and waved her farewell until I could no longer see her in the rearview mirror. I left the driver's window down and waved back as I drove away. Mama was now old and I couldn't help wonder if it would be the last time I would see her alive.

I headed toward my old friend Scotty's house as I pondered her words. That Curry had never said a word to her about her children just didn't sound right. How could he never even ask her about it? I arrived at Scotty's home and we talked for a few minutes.

I rested as Scotty left to go and get Reno and bring him to his home for our meeting. When I heard them drive up, I went out to meet Reno, who was slow in working his way out of the truck. Reno toddled toward the house as I greeted him. I couldn't help but notice the sharp contrast between his appearance now and how I remembered him as a boy. The years had etched their toll upon his face, and his back was slightly bent over from pain and age. However, his good nature and character still shone through.

"Well, goot gracious, how you doin' my boy? That's a mighty fine car you driving," he said, looking at my old '95 Mercedes. Reno liked Mercedes.

"How you doing, Reno?" I replied.

"Good, my boy, you know, good," he said. His voice hadn't changed at all—a strong, deep, and clear timbre as it had always been. His mind was also clearly still very sharp.

We made our way into the house and took a seat at the counter. I motioned to Scotty that we needed a few minutes alone, and he left. I put all my cards on the table.

"Reno, I need some answers, and you're the only person that can give them to me. Can I ask you some direct questions?"

"Oooohhh, yeaaaahhh, my boy. You know you can ask me anything," he said.

As I gazed at him, I felt like a little boy again. But this time there was something missing: many years had slipped by and I was no longer a boy.

"Reno, did Percy talk to you much about me and Tammy?" I asked him.

"Oh yea, we talked about ever'thang," he said.

"Scotty told me that you can quote poetry and you are a good reader."

"Oh yea, dat why Mr. Percy hired me so I could read all his papers. You know Mr. Percy couldn't read too good."

I went forward with the next question. "Do you know when Curry found out that Percy was my father?"

"Oh yea, he knew all along, he shaw did," Reno said.

"How did he live with knowing that Percy was me and Tammy's real father?" I couldn't help but ask.

Reno looked at me, considering for a long moment.

"I'm gone tell you something, Dino. Mr. Percy was a direct man, you know dat. When ya mama was carr'ing you, Mr. Percy took Curry aside and told him that you was his and that they ain't a damn thang that he gonna do 'bout it. And if anybody was gone leave then, his ass could hit the road but he won't gonna say nothing 'bout it to ya mama, not one word ever. And you know Mr. Percy meant every word of it."

I stared at Reno in disbelief, thinking that this explained why Mama said that Curry never said a bad word about it to her. I was still curious.

"How do you know this?" I asked Reno.

"Cause I was dare when he said it, Dino. That was when I just held my head down and felt sorry for poor ole Curry. You know, Perry, that I tole you when you were little that I just felt sorry for poor ole Curry and dat's why. When Mr. Percy would talk shit, I'd just hang my head down and feel sorry for Curry and think poor, poor ole Curry. Man, I don't know how he did it."

"Me neither, Reno."

Percy Flowers holding young
Perry while Ole Curry walks past
in the background

"But what about Percy's wife? Did she know all along?" I asked.

"Ooooooooh, yeeeaaaaaaah, she knowed. Mr. Percy said it right to her. In the store one day Mr. Percy was tellin' a man that you and Tammy was his children, right in front of ole Curry and Ms. Delma told him be quiet talking like dat in front of Curry. Percy was standin' right dare, referring to Curry," he said. "Percy's reply to her was, 'Oh, you better shut up at me, you know it's the truth and him, too, and he pointed to Curry. Yes sar, they both knowed it, and they all knowed it around there, shaw did."

"Why doesn't Percy's daughter like Tammy and why doesn't she want her on the farm?" I asked.

Reno came back quickly to this. "She don't like neither one of you, you nor Tammy."

"Why not?"

"Well, dat's just dat ole shit in her head, and I gone tell you why. She use to watch her mama sit at dat window up dare and she saw all the hurt her mama went through over you children. Her mama seen Mr. Percy and me riding you children round and playing over dare at the store. Sometimes she would tell me, now I saw you over dare t'day playing with them children, Howard. Yes sar, she knew all the time. And dat's why her daughter don't like y'all."

I tried to collect my thoughts as I listened to Reno. I thought how cold and wrong it all must have seemed to his wife and daughter.

"She went through hell back then and there wasn't nothing she could do," I said.

"Dat's right, Dino." He nodded.

I told Reno that Tammy and I could not help the circumstances of how we were born into this world and that we didn't have a choice in the matter. She shouldn't be mad at us—we couldn't help it nor change it. In fact, I felt empathy and compassion for Percy's wife and daughter. They were victims in their own way, just as we were, and because of the same events and circumstances.

"Yea, dat's just dat ole shit in her head from seeing her mama hurt so much. Naw, sir, it ain't right but dat's how it is, my boy."

Scotty returned and Reno shared the information with him as well, as if finally to say, *I'm not afraid to speak out any longer.* Reno knew how wrong it all had been, but he was never able to say anything to anyone, especially in those days. That night, Reno continued to tell us stories of those times, almost as if venting and then inhaling a new breath.

I had lived all my life in the shadows of Percy Flowers's legacy, restricted from all legitimate right by virtue of namesake. I always remained silent as people boasted of his legendary lifestyle, as they had no clue his very son was standing right before them. I considered that my children might not ever be able to freely visit the farm or be honest about who they were. They might never be able to openly claim their legacy to the king of moonshining, Joshua Percy Flowers. Even to this day, people still tell tales about the legendary Percy Flowers and his rule over the enormous illicit whiskey kingdom.

But, I asked myself, was it right to open all the old wounds? Or was it fair that I continue to live with the secret, fearful to openly pronounce my blood right to Percy Flowers?

Generations to come would never know the truth if I took it with me to my grave. Could it cost me or my family our livelihoods to tell the truth? My vigor to own an empire and be like Percy had long been overridden by a desire for knowledge, wisdom, compassion, and understanding. I enjoyed each day at a time and found the simple pleasures in life as I had witnessed Percy's hardship as he strived to earn a dollar until the final days of his life.

Percy had left this earth just like ole Curry and every other man that ever lived. James's biblical writings came to mind: "We are just a mist and are gone." My wife of twenty years had guided me and helped me understand what had happened. She had demonstrated patience and kindness and taught me how to lead a productive life while dealing with all the ghosts of the past. But knowing my past legacy and remaining silent would give rise to yet another set of victims, Percy's grandchildren. Since these are my own sons whom I love, I would not treat them as I had been treated.

Percy Flowers believed in bloodline in every sense of the word. Yet there are two children and grandchildren who come from his bloodline but may never bear his name. When I left the store on our vacation and said goodbye to Reno, I wrestled with what was right and determined it was my duty to end this secret forever. I decided to expose the hidden truths that consumed me, once and for all.

His grandchildren will know their legacy! They will know their grandfather, my father, was not perfect by any means, but he did what he had to do to survive in hard times. He was not formally educated but cannily self-taught. They will know that he was a moonshiner and bootlegger. He was a farmer, foxhound racer, and cockfighter. He was chivalrous and spoke his mind. He believed in helping people, usually the least among us, and did so often. They will know that he was full of life and loved living. They should never be fearful or embarrassed at their blood right to Percy Flowers. They should be able to stand before their grandfather's grave and know the truth.

As I drove away and came to all these realizations, they were hard to bear, not just for me, but for the other victims as well.

17

VICTIMS

Dear Josh and John,

Secrets often produce victims. The problem with se-crets is that they rarely remain secrets if more than one per-son knows. Quite often the victims suffer and pay the price for those acts. It would be difficult to gauge who suffered most or who was most deeply scarred over the affair that bore two children so very long ago. In this case, the truth is, there were five such victims: Curry, Percy's wife and daugh-ter, my sister Tammy, and, of course, me.

It was the mid-1960s and I was just a boy. We still lived in the old white plank house. Mama sat on our blue cloth couch next to Percy as he told me, "You know, you my boy, Perry. You the las' button off Ole Gabe's coat."

Even then, the questions were already swirling both in my mind and the minds of others as to the secret of my identity. Like most secrets, when more than one person knows, then it isn't a secret for very long. In this case, the secret was revealed shortly after Mama found out she was pregnant. Of course, she had to share this with Percy, and it came as no surprise. After all, they were actually *trying* to have a child together.

Mama had been married to Curry for over fifteen years and had not conceived. She was desperate for children and Curry couldn't father any as the mumps had gone down on him. Percy's only legitimate son, Percy Jr., had been tragically killed in the plane crash. Percy Jr.'s two young children were then whisked away from the area by their mother to shield them from the danger of the moonshining business. Their absence had left an empty spot in Percy's soul.

Yes, the affair between Percy and my mother would leave lifelong scars on its victims.

Poor ole Curry was the first victim, and he suffered as much as anyone. He lived with the knowledge from the very beginning. He bore the heavy cross of knowing all along that Percy was my father. Every morning he arose to the same old routine to work at the store that Percy owned. He drove down the same dirt path to the store to stand behind the counter all day until 9:00 p.m., over fourteen hours per day. Then he drove the same path in reverse to return home and sleep. He was like a rented horse that walked the same path, returning to the stall only to do it all again the next day. He had only one day off per week, Thursday. Percy owned Curry. Being Curry's boss and giving Curry's wife children that Curry could not himself produce, Percy basically had domain of all the meaningful aspects of a man's life: his woman and his work.

Curry's words were few to me growing up, and his love, if he had any, was also silent, vaulted tightly within his heart. He never, even once, played a game of catch or did any type of father-son activity. I thought that was just how it was. He was just there to go to work. His face always looked the same, with rarely a smile or laugh, a mask he held expressionless most of the time. From behind the store counter, he witnessed his own body age and decline. All of his aspirations, if he ever had any, slowly faded into the darkness of his own mind.

Curry must have allowed the secret to consume his soul and then his work to consume his time. For over thirty-five years he worked for Percy. There were no sick days, retirement, or benefits. He just worked day after day for $300 per month. I never heard him complain, not even once, his entire life all but a hateful lie. Curry worked at the store until Percy's death in 1982. Mama and Curry separated not long after. It was her doing. Without any savings or retirement, he moved to Rock Ridge, North Carolina, and continued to work. I stayed in touch with Curry through the years and realized the hardship that he had endured. We built a fragile relationship.

In 1996, he moved to the Midwest to live with my family for four years on our farm. We became friends. During these four years he seemed happy. I owned a small business in the local town, and he spent his days sitting around the store and going places with me. I once mentioned God to him, and he seemed bitter toward religion and God. Around 2000, I moved to Texas to fly with a major airline. Of course we invited Curry to go with us. He respectfully declined, wanting to move back to an area near his relatives. He said that he was getting too old to keep moving. His last move to North Carolina was to a government-assisted retirement apartment. During his last years, he lived alone. His body was frail, and he walked with a cane. I visited him several times a year, treating him as if he were my only father and intentionally avoiding any hint of the event. Curry and I would visit friends or relatives and just enjoy the days.

In December 2006, at the retirement home, he said, "I've outlived just about ever'body from my time and I got it the best now I've ever had it in my life. I enjoy every day now."

This was the only time I can ever remember him sharing his personal feelings with me. It was like some miraculous healing had fallen from the heavens without warning. He said very few words, but they had great meaning this time. He seemed content and happy. For him, I believe the pain of the dark secret was over and done with. I was glad that he had found peace in his last days.

As he lay dying in the Smithfield Memorial Hospital, I sat by his side there in Room 311, and we talked about many things and people. While morphine entered his veins to relieve the pain of a damaged back and physical decay, he occasionally talked of the past as if reliving it. He spoke of the year 1948 and also President Truman's presidency. He spoke of people from his childhood. At times his mind was as sharp as ever.

As difficult as it was, I could not let him pass without knowing for sure.

"Did you know all along about Percy being my father?" I finally asked.

He replied with a head nod while he kept his eyes closed as if he could not bear the pain. I let it go at that. He knew others knew of his shame, but he didn't speak of it. His voice had been silenced in 1961 when my mama began to show that she was pregnant for the first time. What other person could bear so much and with quiet fortitude?

My sister Tammy was just seventeen years old and still at an impressionable age when Percy died. The rug had been quickly pulled out from under her. Percy had been the cornerstone of her life and served as a father figure even though she did not live under the same roof. She depended upon him entirely. She was left alone—stripped of her sense of security and financial support while all that she'd trusted was gone like a night star that had burned out and vanished. Tammy was a young woman and beautiful, just like her half sister, but dirt poor. She was devastated at Percy's death and as she watched our half sister inherit the entire farm as we were left to fend for ourselves.

Our mother, Bea, did the best she could to raise her children, but she did not know how to properly model a "normal relationship" for Tammy. Thus, Tammy's only model was the dysfunctional and twisted relationship between

Percy, Bea, and Curry. Percy's death left Tammy to fend for herself as she struggled with the demons of abandonment. Her knowledge of the affair left Tammy deeply scarred, even though she loved her mother and Percy.

Tammy was extremely intelligent and hard working. After she served her time in the navy, she worked her way through college and earned a degree in early childhood education. She taught school for several years and then pursued a successful career with a major communications firm. Seemingly calm, normal, and beautiful on the outside, her mind suffered tormenting demons from Percy's death and sudden departure. The affair and the secrecy of our identity robbed her of trust and commitment. Her mental state, when it came to trusting men, was damaged and in desperate need of repair. Her relationships with men were subsequently always rocky, as jealousy seemed to prevail as the dominant trait in any relationship.

Many times I watched her struggle with the rage of trusting someone when she so wanted to but couldn't— and she didn't seem to understand why. She believed that all men were untrustworthy and would ultimately let her down in some way. What an unfortunate view of life for any soul. In the early years Tammy was drawn to abusive relationships, and when she found a loving person, it seemed she sabotaged the relationship without reason. With professional help, she came to understand the damage that her dysfunctional upbringing had done to her. She came to see that her lack of self-worth meant that in her mind she never deserved a normal relationship. As a result, she continues to work diligently to preserve her marriage and not repeat the mistakes of the past. She has done well and continues to be a role model to her son. Her husband is also a caring and steady person making the three of them a wholesome family. Tammy took on the full-time responsibility of caring for her aging mother. This is yet another noble task that she alone deserves credit for. Overall she is a survivor.

*Perry and Tammy Sullivan as
young children*

Who were the other victims? I can only speculate based upon Percy's accounts, my mother's testimony, and Reno's words what misery Percy's wife and daughter bravely endured. Percy's wife, Delma, was a respected member of the community and church, a kind and gentle woman who always treated me well the few times we talked. Delma was above snide remarks or any ill gestures toward innocent children but must have felt pain as she sat at that window right there on the farm and watched her husband raise and play with children who were born of another woman. Even though she knew the secret (as Percy even on occasion boasted about it), she could do nothing about it.

Becky, Percy and Delma's daughter, was also a victim. According to Reno, even though she was just a young girl, she understood the wrongness of what her father had done and the hurt it caused her mother. She was embarrassed by the alleged moonshining operation. It was normal for Becky to blame and despise us as we were the source of her mother's pain. I cannot help but think that the entire state of affairs was ugly and painful for everyone, especially a young daughter. Becky was cheated of a relationship with two siblings who could have been lifelong family and support for her. I, for one, wanted to remain true to Percy's words: "You know she's your half sister, don't you forget it now, Perry." I remembered this and, in my heart, remained loyal and compassionate.

Becky deserves credit for singlehandedly transforming the Flowers Farm into a thriving community and a place far removed from the harsh days of moonshining. Her character and reputation as a strong businesswoman has shone through for over thirty years while she's built the area into a respectable and desirable community. She could have easily sold off all of the farm and lived an easy life of incredible luxury. But that isn't what she was made of. She was made from ole Percy's DNA—and you are who you are. Her drive and resourcefulness have been the trademark of her success.

As for me, how deep my wounds go cannot be measured. There is no gauge or words to describe such pain. Those boyhood years on the farm forged my mind, body, heart, and soul, developing ideas and thought patterns that frame the worldview and perspective for everything I would encounter in life. I knew from a young age that the affair was wrong and did not condone it. I felt compassion for Delma and Becky and never took any action to challenge the lack of an inheritance even though I was encouraged to do so. Even a lifetime of formal education and life experiences that dwarf those times on the farm cannot completely remove the mindset of mistrust and insecurity that are my constant companions. Even though I have already lived a life full in love, academic achievement, and community involvement far beyond expectations, uncertainty shadows me—a feeling of emptiness, a feeling that something is missing. It's not a lack of love or faith, just a lack of closure.

The notorious Percy Flowers, my father, left unfinished business that can never be completed. Percy was right when he told me, as we sat so long ago on that wooden bench in front of the store, that those childhood days were the best of my life. But he failed to warn me of the hardships that would eventually follow. The ghosts of those times would haunt me forever. Perhaps he knew difficult times would come soon enough without dwelling on them.

I knew that I possessed the king's traits of determination and drive. Just like a fighting cock or foxhounds, some traits are just there, and I can't help that. But why didn't he take care of us? And why didn't we have the Flowers last name? My mind was always filled with questions, what ifs and why nots.

In the years following Percy's death, many people were uncertain about what the future would hold. But there is one thing I am absolutely certain of. That is, you are who you are. Nothing can change that. As with a birthday gift, a person is wrapped to look a certain way on the outside, but you rarely know what will be on the inside. You can never know a person's mind, nor their

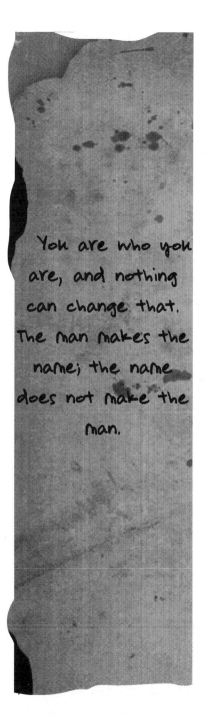

You are who you are, and nothing can change that. The man makes the name; the name does not make the man.

heart. I chose to keep the name "Sullivan" in honor of poor ole Curry, who courageously remained quiet and restrained throughout his life. I firmly believe the man makes the name, the name does not make the man. No matter my name, I would always be the same individual. My identity, by name's sake, Flowers, is lost forever, but Percy's heritage continues through me and my two sons.

I am a firm believer in education, faith, and a healthy dose of practical common sense and good hard work. Although education alone is no guarantee for success, regardless of your background, education will broaden your thinking and will open doors that would never otherwise open. A good education must be tempered by hard work and common sense. As Percy rightly observed, "You can be educated and have no sense." Imagine how unfortunate the soul who has neither education nor sense!

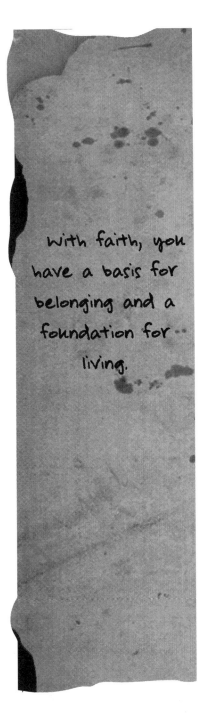

With faith, you have a basis for belonging and a foundation for living.

Mama was not educated, but she had a great deal of sense, and I learned she was right when she told me, "All you need is God and an education."

And that brings me to the final and most important point.

Faith in God is imperative. With faith, you have a basis for belonging and a foundation for living. At times, my sons, you may get lost or drift from the "true North Star" that is faith, but like a beacon, it will always light your path and help you find your way back home.

18

THE SEED OF TRUTH AND FAIRNESS

Dear Josh and John,

You should know more about Howard, the friend and mentor I called Reno. He was more than a whiskey maker and bootlegger. He was a man who lived in hard times, especially for blacks. He set the high standard that I pass on to you when it comes to equality among people. This is not to say all are equal or deserve equality but to say fairness should thrive and be practiced among all men regardless of color. If all men could be like Reno, then color would not matter.

Reno, the whiskey man, was a good and pure soul, born in a time and place where white meant the Ku Klux Klan and black was spelled nigger with a capital N. Everybody had a place and a black man was the workhorse of endless laborious days. By God, many believed, "if a nigger had any rights, it was the rights his boss gave to him and that was as good as being handed the Ten Commandments." Don't be offended by the bluntness of the times, that's just the way it was then, and I know it because I saw it and lived through it. It didn't make a difference how good or right a black man was because it was all up to the boss and the boss did the almighty judging. A mangy, flea-covered dog might get better treatment than some black people when it came to some of the white folk of the time.

Howard was a true friend to me, a black symbol of hope whom I knew as Reno. From the time I was born, Reno was there at the store, a man whom I saw as good and hard-working. He took a lot of shit by just "grinning and bearing it" because he knew he was no match for the swift justice of the white folks of that era.

Percy and others had a deep respect for Reno and would do almost anything for him, but even a boss who showed too much kindness to a black might be seen as a weak sympathizer at a time when whites, too, were punished for such things. It was an ugly form of cultural or peer pressure. Sometimes even the bosses were forced to be cruel out of loyalty to the "way things have always been."

Reno was up as high on the social ladder as a Negro could be at that place and time and held a trusted position because he belonged to Percy's empire. Nobody messed

with this empire without Percy's permission and this offered Reno a certain status. That was another unwritten,
hard-and-fast law that people just knew and respected.
Reno knew a great deal about Percy's moonshining empire
as he had worked for him in the most secretive parts of the
operation—moonshining and bootlegging.

Reno originally met Percy as a young boy and had always worked for him. As a boy, Reno hid pints of the clear
moonshine in his rubber boots and sold them to customers from the outside of the country store. Percy didn't own
Reno by right of bill of sale like a slave, but Percy did own
Reno. Reno was bound by the knowledge he possessed
from years in the shadowy operation. His job description,
whiskey maker, was unique, and he was at the absolute
top of the game for his profession.

Being a whiskey man with Percy was as good as it got.
Still, Negros had their place and they knew it. Reno was
wise and knew when to listen and when to speak. He was
very keen in that sense and that is probably why he lasted
so long. I learned from Reno that sometimes the path of
least resistance is the best path. After all, the fiery trails
blazed by some of the most aggressive people were quickly
snuffed out and forgotten. To challenge the degrading comments blacks suffered would only have ended in abuse,
death, or other loss.

One day at the store, a man walked in and mentioned
that he'd heard that Percy had purchased an outside wood-
fired heating system for his home. The man commented
that it must be quite a job to keep it fired with wood.

"Hell, I got a nigger that can fire a boiler better than anybody, it ain't no trouble at all," Percy replied. He was referring to my friend, Reno.

"Yes sar, yes sar, I shaw can, that I can," Reno said. I was just a young boy, but that comment lit me on fire inside and I never forgot it. I felt sorry for Reno as I saw him reply with a smile almost as if Percy had paid him a compliment. Compliment or not, this kind of talk made me mad and I knew that I would never treat a person like that no matter their race.

The term "nigger" was commonly used and accepted then by both black and white folk. Nonetheless, it didn't feel right. "Nigger" was not that bad compared to some other words and treatments dealt to Negros. But imagine today saying in a crowd of people, "Tell that nigger over there to get busy!" This would incite a riot.

Reno lived in Smithfield and drove his old, '60s-model maroon Ford Fairlane to the store every day, seven days a week. There were no days off for Reno. Moonshining was his work and the lifebreath of his existence. He worked for Percy full time and this meant from around seven in the morning to nine thirty at night—and any other time he was needed.

Reno's old Fairlane was always followed by a blue smoke trail. I'd ask Reno why his car smoked so much, and he put the same good humor that he always had in his answer. He said his car put out mosquito smoke to keep the mosquitoes away; it was made like that new from Ford, he explained. If Reno said it, I believed it. I believed that for many years.

"Reno and Dino" (Howard
Creech and Perry Sullivan)
Christmas 2008

After I was five years old, I spent a lot of time at the store, just playing there. Reno often sat around waiting for customers to pull up to the corner of the store for "special service." He also kidded me about going to see a cousin in California.

"Dino," he would say, "go home and get packed. We're going to California to see your cousin."

When I got home, I packed a bag with clothes and prepared for our trip.

Mama scolded me. "Put them clothes back. Howard was teasing with you."

Of course, when I returned to the store, Reno would say, "Dino, I've been waiting for you all this time, what you mean she won't let you go? Goot gracious, I'm going to talk to her."

Meanwhile, I would get mad. When I got home again, I'd tell Mama, "I told you he was going."

This type of horseplay went on for a long time; I'm not even sure for how many years. Sometimes Reno would use his watch as a stopwatch and time me running around the grocery counters and pretend to give me an impressive time, as though I were a true track star. He would make like nobody else could run that fast. I'd stand beside him and say, "Do it again, Reno!" as if I could break another record time. He'd oblige me as long as I wanted. When I asked him to take a turn at running, he would say that he had a bone in his leg and couldn't run. Of course, as a kid, I would argue back that he didn't have any bones in his leg. Just get up and run! Reno and I had a lot of fun.

Reno also helped me to sharpen my driving skills, letting me drive the pickup around the farm. Once Reno needed to go to the Pearsall Farm to check some barrels. It was raining and the dirt roads and paths were muddy. He got us a Pepsi and Baby Ruth and said, "C'mon, my boy, you can drive."

We walked out to a '60s-model, ¾-ton white Ford pickup truck with manual steering and a stick shift. This was a farm pickup in every sense. The truck had mud grips on the back and a built-in toolbox on the side—just the way Ford made it. The bench seat was covered with grain, and the rubber flooring was hidden with dirt. Reno crawled in first and lifted me up onto his lap so that I could drive. He pushed the clutch as he let me start the truck. It was cold and damp, so he had to pat the accelerator to get it to start. The wipers squeaked as they crossed the windshield. The engine warmed up and the heater came on, and we wiped a spot clean on the dew-covered windshield so we could see out.

With me at the wheel and Reno controlling the pedals, we headed toward Archer Lodge drinking Pepsis and eating Baby Ruths. We came upon the small dirt path that went by the old house where we lived and continued to the Pearsall Farm. The path was marred with a rut track and deep mud puddles. Limbs from the trees bowed down and brushed the truck as we bumped down the path. While straddling some deep potholes, the front wheels hopped out of the rut and the truck began to slide and bounce across the path. Reno had my Pepsi in one hand and a Baby Ruth in the other, so he couldn't get to the steering wheel.

"Hang on, Dino, hang on to it, Dino, don't let it get away!" he said. He must have had a lot of confidence in my driving skills.

I wrestled the old truck with all my might and finally steered it back into the rut. The experience truly scared me, but Reno just laughed out loud and said, "I hear you, Dino. Nobody can drive like that."

Reno and me were buddies. I had all the respect in the world for him. Even now I wonder what he really thought of whites and the way blacks were treated then. Even though people often said bad things about Negros, I could never find any bad in him. Never did I hear him say a bad word about a single person. He had a unique talent for making every person feel like his favorite.

But there is an interesting footnote to my story about my good friend, Reno.

Remember the lesson *you can never know what is in a person's heart, you can only know what they let you know?* I believe Reno had more than a few secrets. I remember back to some words that ole Reno said to me later in life as he sat in his apartment watching over the king's throne. He was quite content, as he had been well taken care of since Percy's death and given a place to live and an income to live on.

Reno had a way with words and sometimes spoke in parables. As we sat and discussed how Curry had never said a bad word about the whole affair, Reno, with a peculiar look and slight smile, made two statements that made me think back.

The first was this.

"Poor ole Curry's lips said one thing, but his heart said another. And time has a way of taking care of all thangs, Dino." He told me this with a small head nod and a slight wink as he lightly patted his own heart.

For some reason, my mind flashed back to a day at the store when Percy cussed Reno and yelled at him to "get up there and cover dem damn gallons of whiskey before we all go to jail." Percy and I had seen them exposed as we drove in from Archer Lodge. Reno responded by remaining quiet and showing no emotion and then quickly heading toward the old home place to cover them.

I also thought back to a few days after Percy's death when Reno came by the house and quickly motioned me over to his car as he had parked by the white barn. Reno was pointing at his open wallet so full of money that it bulged, unable to be closed. The hundred-dollar bills were over two inches thick. From the looks of things, he had over fifteen thousand dollars in there. Reno ran his thumb through the hundreds exposing them as to say "all hundreds." I thought that maybe he held the money for the Brown Farm purchase that never materialized—the farm that Percy and Reno were going to purchase in cash the week Percy had died.

Was Percy having Reno conduct one last piece of business?

"What you think about this, m'boy? This just a part of it," he said. Reno, by all accounts, was supposed to be broke.

He left and never explained what any of it was for nor where it had come from. I was a bit surprised that he had so much cash, as Curry had never received any, and by the time Percy had passed away, his cash supply was short and everyone suffered, even Percy's wife and his daughter Becky, according to Curry. There had been barely enough money to run the operation and keep the farm.

"His lips said one thing, but his heart said another," Reno had told me. At the time, I thought he was speaking of Curry's heart, but it dawned on me that perhaps Howard had been speaking of his own. Maybe this was how Reno really felt about the way he'd been treated. Perhaps he regarded the money as repayment for all the humiliation he'd quietly endured through the years.

Regardless of what he meant or did, Reno, my friend Howard, was a powerful role model. Little did I know that he'd planted the seed of fairness and equality in my young mind and that this would ultimately rule out prejudice forever for me. It took time for the seed to grow, but it did and does still. I will be forever grateful to and indebted to my ole friend Reno.

*Howard "Reno" Creech in 1978
(in the background is housing for
the fighting cocks)*

*Reno making scuppernong wine
from grapes we picked*

19

POOR, POOR OLE CURRY

Dear Josh and John,

So often we are quick to judge or misjudge. Based on a first impression, or on just a few words, we miss the opportunity to share a friendship that might be a gift to our lives. What so often seems to be is sometimes not. Ask yourself how far you would go to make another person happy. Would you give up most all of your own life's happiness and dreams for someone else?

I told you that Reno referred to Curry as "poor, poor ole Curry" while holding his head down in pity for him. There was good reason.

Percy, with Reno standing by his side, took Curry aside one day and told him that Bea, my mother, was pregnant from their affair and that a child was to be born. There was one more thing Percy told Curry:

"You won't ever say a thang, not one word, to Bea about it. If you can't live with it, then it will be your ass that has to go."

That's a lot for any man to have to quietly carry around all his life. It was a secret that he was forced to bear. As Bea lay in the Woodard Herring Hospital giving birth, Curry remained at the store working, head held down, muttering contempt. He was filled with fear and hatred from knowing what he knew and was unable to speak of it to Bea. Even expectant mother Bea was never informed that Curry had been taken aside and talked to.

Percy accepted his responsibility as my father and felt he was protecting Bea when he did this. Curry was given the option to leave quietly or to accept his role and stay. Remember, Curry was a simple man, but this is not to say he was simple minded.

One could argue that Percy's ability to wield the sword and own Curry as a part of his moonshining empire was enough to keep Curry grounded to the farm. But I knew Percy and Curry well enough to say that it had to happen the way it did. Even though Percy was fierce as a businessman and moonshiner, he would have allowed Curry to leave without recourse if he had wanted to. But Percy had granted Bea a child and he, too, accepted that role. It was just a matter of whether Curry would accept all of this. Times then were very "matter of fact" without a lot of discussion. I believe that Curry's decision to stay was influenced by that one important force that caused men to do the most out-of-character things: love.

Even though he was silenced before my birth by Percy's threat, Curry was committed to standing by Bea as he had committed to her in their marriage vows "for better or for worse." Curry meant every word of those vows. Everything Curry did had meaning. He stood by his word and meant what he said. He was in love with Bea and knew how much she wanted children. It was bad enough that he couldn't provide them for her, but should he deny her children altogether—children that would bring her joy, happiness, and fulfillment as a mother? Most men would say yes to this moral dilemma. He knew how much she so deeply wanted children and through his own self-sacrifice accepted her affair for the sake of her overall happiness. In his mind, that was love. And he accepted it even though it pained him horribly.

Percy's threat was real, but in Curry's mind petty as he had the bigger picture of Bea's happiness in his heart; he would have stayed with her regardless. Curry saw how happy it made Bea to have her dream come true and he delighted in it. Still, he wasn't sure how to treat a child not his own, and his coldness toward me may have been similar had I been of his own blood. Even though Percy openly announced that Tammy and I were his children, Curry held his temper and dealt with his anger and frustration internally.

Once at the store, Percy's wife Del asked Curry how he felt about those children being Percy's. He simply said, "I'm raising them, and as far as I'm concerned, they are mine."

Curry held to his commitment as a man and a father the best that he knew how. Reflecting upon the past, it would be fair to say that his actions could have been much worse.

Later in life, Curry lived with my family for several years, and I learned a lot about him. Curry was not a leader. In fact, he didn't have an ounce of leadership in his whole body. He was a follower in every way. He was not even able to speak clearly most of the time. He mumbled as if ashamed of his own voice. Some even thought he had some speech problem. Most of the time he was quiet. He was un-educated and considered coarse. I never saw much in him as a child because of his coldness toward me.

For many years I held Curry in contempt for being a pitiful father, void of any love or affection. Never once did we do a single thing as father and son. No baseball, no fishing, no movie, no nothing. Mama said she had to make him get me a Christmas gift when I was a boy. Even as the years passed and Curry grew old and fragile, he remained mostly quiet. I realized that I had misjudged Curry. He was simply not able to express himself. He had never been taught to do so.

Curry showed love in the most subtle ways. Like his words, his actions were few but meant a great deal. Even though he showed no affection to me, he never criticized me or dissuaded me in any way—never. Curry was simply quiet. That was his way. He knew that time had a way of healing and dealing with situations. He had come up during the Depression and was used to hard times his whole life. You might say his best friend was disappointment. He was able to put the past behind him on a daily basis and looked forward to the next day for a new chance. Curry was able to find happiness in simple pleasures.

Once at my store in the Midwest, he motioned me over to sit and observe a squirrel that was up in a tree eating an acorn.

"Just look at that squirrel enjoying the day!" he observed.

He also enjoyed watching my sons playing. Once I said to him, "That is a cute little rascal!" referring to my son.

He replied with a smile. "You know, when they're cute little, they grow up not to be so cute."

That was not an insult. It was, in fact, a rare and simple attempt at humor.

Curry also possessed unmatched strength and restraint. When we spoke of Percy and the days on the farm, he always picked out some pleasant moment to talk about; he spoke never a bad word about anyone.

For the entire time he lived with me in his later years, we enjoyed one another's company, and I came to love Curry as a father and respect him as a man. I learned that he was very smart and understood people and life very well. His simple ways of dealing with life rubbed off on me. I just wish that I could have learned from him during my childhood. He taught me forgiveness, understanding, and, most of all, patience. He did what he said he would do. He never had much of anything, but he managed to find strength to carry on for ninety-two years without so much as a negative word about anyone.

Curry was more of a man than anyone I will ever meet. He endured without criticizing and walked in strength. If all the people of the world had an ounce of his tolerance and patience, the world would be a better place. To a man so misunderstood and so underappreciated, I most humbly apologize and ask forgiveness for ever saying or even thinking a single bad thing about him.

Curry has truly become a beacon of light to me. Never have I known a person of such strength and restraint. Rest in peace, Curry.

Curry (Willis) Sullivan

20

MOVING FORWARD

Dear Josh and John,

As I sit by a warm fire tonight and observe the tall Christmas tree with all the gifts resting underneath, I think how lucky we are. It is nearly Christmas. It is a time of year to be thankful for what you have, not what you could have had or should have had but what you actually have. For me, this is a time to reflect on another year passing and all the years past. It is a time to reflect on the gifts of life. It is a time for yet another story or letter to you.

It is quiet tonight as you boys are finally asleep. I close my eyes, listen to the fire crackle, and remember all the way back to when I was five years old and Percy visited our home on that cold winter's day.

I remember the excitement of giving him the Hai Karate aftershave and how his beard felt as he rubbed it against my face with a smile. I recall the sound of his voice as he asked me, "Whose boy are you, Perry?"

I reminisce about the many times we sat on the old wooden bench—the "bench of knowledge"—as he talked to me as a son, as a boy, and as a friend. I think back to the many times that we rode around in the big Cadillacs and dog trucks, our minds filled only with thoughts of hunting. The simple days playing at the store and watching all the old timers come by and just talk about nothing.

I think of the difficult times when I looked upon Percy for the last time before the coffin lid closed, ending my life and that of my sister and mother as we knew it. I think of the feeling of loneliness and abandonment after his death.

Percy passed, taking with him only what he'd arrived with. His life was filled with strife from earning a dollar. It was his nature. He was driven to succeed, rarely slowing to find simple pleasure. His mission was to change the world that he lived in, and he did so. He gulped down the goblet of life as fast as he could. He worked at that pace all the way to the end.

I also remember Reno as a young man, when his voice was deep, his back was straight, and his laugh comforting. We had so much fun driving the farm trucks and drinking sodas on hot summer days. I can see it clearly, the little giant jumping as the clear moonshine ran from the copper pipe and we caught it in a bucket. He looked up with a nod of his head and a kind smile, knowing that he was teaching me an old trade.

I remember back to the recent visit with Reno when he informed me of Percy laying down the law to ole Curry. His back wasn't so straight anymore and his face was written with the many years of his life. He was ready to open the attic windows and blow out all the old cobwebs and air out the place. He was relieved to be at a point in life that he could talk openly about the past without recourse, as he knew I would keep my word and stay quiet until the time came to tell the story.

Reno taught me how to have fun and be funny. He was a strong role model, but he never realized it at the time. His lightheartedness and love of people—all races—taught me to look for the best in all folks. Reno has been that role model to countless children throughout the years. He is forever respected by so many.

I also can't help but think of poor ole Curry standing behind the register day after day, year after year, and how I had misjudged him for so long. His sober look was constant. I remember him bringing home the red alligator-skin AM/FM radio on Christmas around 1965. I think back to his commitment to Bea and us children as he did the best that he knew how to do. He was so tolerant to come home to us each night after the long days of work. Ole Curry never said a bad thing to Mama, and he never once discouraged or criticized us children. I think back to his time in later years as I grew to know him as a man. His simple ways and words I miss so very much. I remember just before he died. He came to me in a dream. His lips and gums were purple. He stood still in front of me, looking straight ahead with a very faint smile as he stretched his right arm forward and opened his hand. He handed me his own father's golden pocket watch. I had for-gotten about that watch but then remembered it from when I was just a boy. He kept it in an old steel safe in the closet. The dream felt as if he were saying goodbye and passing the time on to me. He displayed very little emotion, but he was at ease. He died the next day, eyes looking forward with his life all behind him. He had finally found peace.

Sure, Curry was never recognized for much of any-thing. His quiet ways always went unnoticed. He stood before others while Percy openly acknowledged me as his own. He listened quietly without argument or fight. He found life's simple pleasures and knew how to enjoy them. As we became friends, I cherished his mild character and how he could say so much by saying so little. He taught me how to be patient. In the end, his life was full.

I remember my mother as the one constant in a child-hood riddled with questions. She was always firm in faith and consistent in patience and support. She knew the im-portance of a good education and how necessary it was to escape the hard way of life so many others around us had experienced.

Mama's prayer that I leave that farm and get away from that way of life was answered and served as the foundation for a strong and broad education. It allowed me to become acquainted with the world and to meet challenges that enriched my life far more than her imagination could ever have dreamed. Her faith and persistent motherly guidance made all the difference in the world for us children. There is no replacement for a caring mother.

As I reflect on my role as the unacknowledged son of Percy Flowers, the son that was, by all accounts, lost, as far as the name Flowers, I am certain that he knew that over time, all this would work out just fine in the end. He knew that I had, as he referred to so often, "what it takes." He knew that no matter the hardships I would face, I would do what was necessary to prepare for what lay ahead.

Nothing was left to me through a will that seemed outdated by all accounts. The farm that he and Reno were going to purchase for my family was blocked by his untimely death, and the money vanished. I was abandoned before his body lay cold in the ground. But he knew that the recipe for survival lay not in material gifts but in the DNA—the blood—*I inherited from him. He was a shrewd person by all accounts and knew what role bloodline played in a human being's makeup. It is true that I have inherited something far more valuable than anything he could have left on paper. I inherited his bloodline. I inherited his will, his grit, his keen sense of determination, his energy, and his self-made smarts. I inherited his wisdom and his life lessons, as taught to me on the bench of knowledge and through our many adventures together. All of these have been my inheritance and my true wealth.*

This brings me to the most important point of all. We are the Lost Flowers by name's sake only, as I am the direct bloodline son to the moonshine king, Percy Flowers. You two boys are his direct descendants—his grandsons. You can go forward and know the story of who you are and your legacy. It is my hope that this secret has been laid to rest and you can know the truth before it is lost with time.

AMEN

27351423R00193

Made in the USA
Lexington, KY
05 November 2013